P9-CEK-118

Bakin' Without Eggs

Bakin' Without Eggs

DELICIOUS EGG-FREE

DESSERT RECIPES

FROM THE HEART

AND KITCHEN OF A

FOOD-ALLERGIC FAMILY

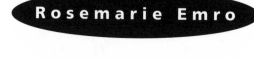

Rosemarie Emro

ST. MARTIN'S GRIFFIN ✿ *NEW YORK*

To our daughter, Caitlin Emro, whose severe egg and peanut allergies inspired the creation of this book.

BAKIN' WITHOUT EGGS. Copyright © 1999 by Rosemarie Emro. All rights reserved. Printed in the United States of America. For information, address St. Martin's Press, 175 Fifth Avenue, New York, N.Y. 10010.

Design by Pei Loi Koay

Library of Congress Cataloging-in-Publication Data
Emro, Rosemarie.
Bakin' without eggs : delicious egg-free dessert recipes from the heart
and kitchen of a food-allergic family / Rosemarie Emro.—
1st St. Martin's Griffin ed.
p.   cm.
ISBN 0-312-20635-6
1. Egg-free diet Recipes.   2. Food allergy—Diet therapy Recipes.
3. Baking.   I. Title.   II. Title: Baking without eggs.
RM232.E47   1999
616.97'50654—dc21
99-14503
CIP

Contents

Acknowledgments

MY SINCERE THANKS to the many people who were involved in this endeavor, from tasting and testing to advising and encouraging.

Very special thanks to my husband, Kevin; my daughter, Caitlin; her pediatrician, Dr. Norman Weinberger; her allergists, Dr. Robert Biondi and Dr. Maryanne Scott; my mother, Maria Mete; my aunt, Jane Emro; Beth Tatto; and to my in-laws Burton and Patricia Emro for their support. Thanks to my agent, Jeanne Fredericks; to my editor, Marian Lizzi and also to Anthony Handal, Esq., for their input and support.

I would like to extend thanks to all the people who tested and tasted recipes for me: my relatives, Margaret and Nancy, Aunt Sally and Tracey Emro, Joe Mango, Sharon and Shawn Kane, John Emro, Maureen and Ned Slawson, Phyllis and Mike Parillo, Melissa, Ann and Andy Ross, John, Ann, Anthony, Margaret, Uncle Sal, and Aunt Marge Mete, Aunt Anna and Larry Guarnieri, Aunt Mary, Uncle Mike, Lisa, Ronnie, Joey and Dianna Paladino, Lisa and Joe Rievecchio, Angela Veschio, Gramma, Uncle Carmine, Aunt Anna and Nick Cioffi, and Aunt Dotty Nocero. My neighbors: Miles and Jodi Wallace, Lori Dunn, Millie Hull, Marie Ottaviano, Annie and Buzzie Parrish, Doreen and Mike Weil, Josie Tucker, Kathleen and Rob Slutz, Bunnie, Ed and Pam Thompson, Judy Tucker, JoAnn and Mike Talercio, JoAnn Perry, Wave Issurdatt, Kathy Mulgano, Lisa and Tony Fiscella. St. Thomas Church: Monsignor William J. Scheyd, Reverend Michael F. Flynn, and Father Murphy. All my daughter's play group and school parents and friends; Cindy Amarel, Joyce Morris, Mary Kennedy, Eunice Tao, Betty Joe Buly, Betty Green, Pat Romanos, Maureen, Danny and Liz Lyons, Marie Sloan, Sharon Soltes, Peggy and Julie Ceponis, Mary Kindle, Harriet Corbo, Sue Ameer, Sara Veno, Denise Denardo, Shiela Freitag, Pauline, and Dr. Nancy Gamer, Liz Ness, Vernice and Carl Holmes, Linda Zampino, Julie Bitar, Pat Bassett, Sally Lawson, Robin Florio, Maria Rievecchio, Linda Chetta, Fran Balestrieri, Kathy Nicholson, Beth Duff, Sharon Esposito, Donna Pappas, Flori, Wally, Vallerie, Jan and Theresa Clarke, Sandy Resnick, RN, the Pediatric Ward at the Norwalk Hospital and its nutritionists, the staff at Dr. Weinberger's and Dr. Biondi's offices, Dr. Bertram Grossman and Dr. Jeanne M. Marconi. Thanks to Jill Tortorella and her daughter Melody, Barbara Harrington, Kathy Hornyak, JoAnn Walsh, Meg Doyle, Patti Krupnik, Pauline Bigica, Liz Norris, Lisa Castorina, Caroline Tibbett, Gabrielle Charette, Mary Balkun, Mary West, Yolanda Ryan, Julie White, June Shutz, Theresa White, Angela Longo, Rudy and Holly Nadilo have my thanks, as well as Mrs. Patricia Dielman, Mrs. Chen, Mrs. Caporrino, and Mrs. Gilman and her whole kindergarten class.

ForeWord

Kevin Emro

IF YOU HAVE FOOD-RELATED ALLERGIES, you will probably empathize with us when you read what I am about to share with you. If you do not have food-related allergies, then you will at least be able to understand why, and how, this cookbook was written.

When our first child, Caitlin, was ready to drink from a bottle, my wife looked forward to it. However, the change was going to prove to be more difficult than we imagined, as we discovered that Caitlin had an allergy to milk products. Thus, we were limited as to the brands of formula we could give her. In addition, she would be drinking formula for a longer period of time than "normal."

One of the first foods our daughter ate, when she was six months old, was pastina. To our horror, she broke out in hives all over her body. After rushing her to the hospital, we were informed by the examining doctor that she had had an allergic reaction, probably to the egg in the pastina she ate. Naturally, we were told not to give her any food containing egg.

We were soon to discover that the *consumption* of egg was not Caitlin's only allergy. This discovery came about after being kissed on her cheek by my wife after she had eaten an egg sandwich. As it turned out, she was also "touch-sensitive" to eggs. This meant that the mere touching of an egg on her skin (or a product containing egg) was sufficient to cause a severe allergic reaction. The medical term for this reaction is *anaphylactic shock,* which causes breathing to shut down and can be fatal. We were astounded to learn that even a very tiny exposure would cause such a reaction.

With the knowledge that Caitlin has a life-threatening allergy to eggs, we were very hesitant to introduce new foods to her in fear that they would trigger a reaction. This fear was reinforced when she was given peanut butter. My wife gave her a very small "drop" of it on the tip of a teaspoon. Immediately, Caitlin broke out in hives, and she began having difficulty breathing. Fortunately, we had been prepared with emergency medication, and were near a local hospital. From that day on, whenever new foods were introduced that were known to be relatively high on the allergy list, we gave them to her in the doctor's office, or in the hospital. To our relief, she has not had allergic reactions to new foods given to her since then.

Since that time, we've learned more about Caitlin's situation, and we've become more comfortable with it. Grocery shopping has been an education, a course in reading product labels and understanding the various terms used to describe the ingredients contained within the packages. (If you stop and think of all the food products lining the shelves of the country's supermarkets, you will soon begin to understand the difficulty of selecting foods that meet a rigid criteria for content.) We discovered that most of the products in the snack foods section contained peanut oil. It was obvious Caitlin couldn't eat any of these products. The same was true of the candy section. I soon realized that besides eggs and nuts themselves, the main areas of concern, as far as groceries were concerned, were snack foods, candy, and ice cream (many ice cream products contain egg and/or nut products) and, sometimes, they change their ingredients (always check labels). Many other types of nuts or sunflower seeds, for example, are roasted in peanut oil (so we had to check for that hidden peanut oil). While these are not part of a balanced diet, they do represent a significant portion of a child's experience and cannot be overlooked.

Eating at public restaurants became a real chore. Prior to ordering, we would have to determine how the restaurant prepared its food. It was vitally important for us to ascertain whether the restaurant cooked in vegetable oil or peanut oil. (Many fast food restaurants cook their french fries in peanut oil.) It was also important to find out if oil was used to cook more than one dish. If a restaurant fried a dish coated in egg batter, and then reused the oil for an "eggless" dish, the "eggless dish" would not be truly "eggless" as minute pieces of egg would find their way into the food using a "community oil." Local diners were out of the question, as most of them cook everything on the same cooking surface. Even after determining that the food preparation process met our tests, we would have to provide the waitperson with very specific instructions on how to prepare Caitlin's food.

One of the reasons I wanted to write the foreword to this cookbook is that I want to get the word out that the reluctance of parents to allow their children (and infants) to be touched is more than paranoia. One of the most common forms of transference of germs between people is through the act of touch, such as a handshake. When Caitlin was an infant, total strangers would walk up to her carriage, and try to touch her hands. It often came to people as a shock that I would interfere with their attempts to touch her. However, I had no way of knowing what kinds of germs, chemicals, or oils were on their hands, which they would be transferring to Caitlin by their touch. For people with life-threatening allergies, this can be fatal. Eating a product containing egg or peanuts tends to leave residue on the hand, such as oil from the peanuts, which could be transferred through the act of touching someone. This happened to

Caitlin once. In the normal course of everyday life, the vast majority of people don't realize the potential adverse effects they may have on another person through the mere act of touching them, despite their harmless intentions.

When Caitlin started going to birthday parties, she would bring a cookie (from home, without egg or nuts). She would then come home and ask us what a chocolate cake tasted like. This pulled on our heart-strings, and it got us thinking that perhaps we could create a cake without the eggs commonly found in cake recipes. My wife's father owned a well-known bakery. He was an excellent baker who rarely used recipes. My wife picked up the same talent, and she started experimenting in the kitchen, baking all kinds of desserts and breads. Before she knew it, whenever our daughter was invited to a party, the hostess would ask my wife to bake the cupcakes or the cake because all the little children ended up eating Caitlin's cupcakes and liked hers better than any other.

Why This Book Was Written
Many cookbooks can be found on the shelves of bookstores all over the world. Most are designed around a specific food theme, but this cookbook is different. It was written with the ordinary person in mind, someone whose baking needs require the absence of egg products (as well as peanuts, although in many cases nuts will be optional). While eggless cookbooks can be found, they are in natural food stores, where special ingredients and/or types of flours such as arrowroot or rice are required. This makes the recipes complicated, expensive, and not exactly kid-friendly. All the ingredients used in place of egg in this cookbook can be found at the local grocery store.

The best part about these recipes is that they taste great. The texture of the cakes is the same as cakes with egg, so you don't know anything is missing. Some of the recipes are also dairy-free, and can be made cholesterol and/or fat-free by substituting applesauce for butter/margarine/oil and low-fat by substituting skim milk for whole milk, but the book is concentrated on egg-free and peanut-free foods.

This book is also for anyone who just likes great baking without the fat. There are a lot of recipes here that have little or no fat. For those concerned with fat intake, if any of the recipes call for sour cream, you can substitute low-fat or no-fat sour cream or low-fat or no-fat yogurt.

I sincerely hope that you enjoy the recipes found in this cookbook as much as we have enjoyed them.

Introduction

THIS COOKBOOK HAS MORE THAN 150 delicious mouthwatering, egg-free recipes, and none requires you to buy anything at the health food store as you would with many other allergy cookbooks. It uses regular ingredients you can find at your local food market.

There are 35 million Americans who suffer from food allergies. Eggs and peanuts are very high on the list of offending foods. Normally, many baked goods include eggs. The recipes in this book simply eliminate the eggs, use no egg substitutes, and are just as good as, if not better than, any of your favorite recipes, including some classics, which I've converted to eggless for this book. When my daughter, who is allergic to eggs, would ask if she could eat a brownie or cake, I made sure she would have one just as good or better than the one that contained eggs. For the most part the recipes are very easy and they are not just for the person who cannot tolerate eggs. These recipes are for anyone who wants to cut out eggs and other fats and keep the great taste of home baking. There are some dairy-free, yeast-free, fat-free, and nut-free recipes also. This is the only book of its kind that I am aware of.

This is a very flexible cookbook because many substitutions can be made with good results. Where a recipe calls for oil, butter, or margarine, many bakers have added applesauce, which makes the recipe fat-free as well. Where a recipe calls for milk, many use skim milk and the low-fat or no-fat sour cream and yogurt.

RECOMMENDED SUBSTITUTIONS TO REDUCE OR ELIMINATE FAT

1 cup buttermilk = 1 tablespoon white vinegar or lemon juice added to 1 cup milk (let stand for 5 minutes)

1 cup oil = ¾ to 1 cup applesauce, depending on how moist you like your cakes (if applesauce is not available, apple juice works, especially for heavy fruit cakes)

1 cup margarine/butter = ¾ to 1 cup applesauce (depending on how moist you like your cake)

1 cup milk = 1 cup skim milk

1 cup yogurt = 1 cup low/no-fat yogurt

1 cup sour cream = 1 cup low/no-fat sour cream

Author's Note

THE AUTHOR OF this book is not a dietitian or medical professional. She makes no representations concerning the recipes in this book other than that they are all egg-free at the time of creation. The information in this book is intended to serve as an alternative to normal baking, without the use of eggs, and it is not intended as a substitute for any treatment that may have been prescribed by a physician.

Since some recipes call for packaged goods, whose ingredients may change over time, it is suggested that you verify the ingredient list of all such packages prior to use. I also use unbleached flour because it is more healthful.

Due to differences in atmospheric conditions (such as humidity) in various locations, you may find some recipes require the liquid content to be slightly higher than suggested in the recipe. If this is the case, you may add more liquid to suit your needs.

These recipes are my family's and friends' favorites. I wish to share them with you, and I hope that you can enjoy these recipes as much as we have.

Breads and Biscuits

Applesauce Bran Bread

2 cups unbleached all-purpose
  flour

¼ cup bran or bran cereal

1 teaspoon baking soda

2 teaspoons baking powder

1 teaspoon ground cinnamon

¼ teaspoon ground nutmeg

½ cup firmly packed brown sugar

½ cup honey

1 cup fresh applesauce

½ cup apple juice

1 tablespoon lemon juice

1 cup raisins

This is a hearty, old-fashioned brown bread.

1. Preheat oven to 350°F. Lightly butter a 9 x 5 x 3-inch loaf pan.

2. In a large bowl, combine flour, bran, baking soda, baking powder, cinnamon, nutmeg, sugar, honey, applesauce, apple juice, and lemon juice. With a wooden spoon, mix thoroughly. Fold in raisins.

3. Spoon batter into prepared pan; spread evenly. Bake for 30 to 40 minutes or until golden and a toothpick inserted in center comes out clean.

4. Remove pan from oven onto wire rack. Cool for 10 minutes, then turn onto plate.

NOTE: This bread freezes well for up to 1 month.

Banana Peachy Low-Fat Bread

makes 1 loaf

3 very ripe bananas, mashed

¼ cup orange juice

1 (8-ounce) container peach low-
fat yogurt

¼ cup quick rolled oats

2¼ cups unbleached all-purpose
flour

2 teaspoons baking powder

1 cup sugar

This is a great, healthy, and cakelike snack. My children and their friends love this dessert; it is very moist.

1. Preheat oven to 350°F. Lightly butter and flour a 9 x 5 x 3-inch loaf pan, tapping out excess flour.

2. In a large bowl, add bananas and, with a handheld electric mixer set on low speed, beat until smooth; slowly add orange juice, yogurt, oats, flour, baking powder, and sugar. Mix until batter is smooth.

3. Spoon batter into prepared pan and bake for 50 to 55 minutes or until golden brown.

4. Remove pan to wire rack. Cool 10 minutes before removing bread from pan.

Banana Pistachio Buttermilk Bread

makes 1 loaf

1 cup sugar

⅓ cup butter or margarine, room temperature

1 cup very ripe mashed bananas (2 small bananas)

2 cups unbleached all-purpose flour

1½ teaspoons baking powder

1 teaspoon baking soda

¼ cup skim milk

2 teaspoons white vinegar or lemon juice

½ cup chopped pistachio nuts

This recipe is also delicious without the pistachio nuts, but the nuts give it an unusual flavor that you will love (if you are not allergic to nuts).

1. Preheat oven to 325°F. Lightly butter a 9 x 5 x 3-inch loaf pan.

2. In a large bowl, with a handheld electric mixer set on medium speed, cream sugar and butter or margarine for 1 to 2 minutes until light and fluffy. Slowly add mashed bananas. Add flour, baking powder, baking soda, skim milk, and vinegar or lemon juice one at a time, mixing after each addition. Mix well until combined. Fold in nuts at the end.

3. Pour batter into prepared loaf pan and allow to stand 10 minutes before baking.

4. Bake for 50 to 60 minutes until browned and toothpick inserted in center comes out clean.

5. Remove from oven and cool in pan on wire rack for 10 minutes.

Healthy Heart Banana Bread

½ cup skim milk

1 tablespoon lemon juice

⅓ cup low-fat vanilla yogurt

3 very ripe medium bananas, cut
  up

2 cups unbleached all-purpose
  flour

¼ cup quick rolled oats

1¼ cups sugar

2 teaspoons baking powder

This is a delicious bread for anyone who likes to eat nutritiously.

1. Preheat oven to 350°F. Lightly butter and dust with flour 10-cup Bundt pan or fluted tube pan, tapping out excess flour.

2. In a measuring cup, pour the milk and lemon juice together and set aside for a few minutes.

3. Meanwhile, in a large mixing bowl, with a handheld electric mixer set on medium speed, combine the yogurt and bananas; beat until smooth, add flour, oats, sugar, baking powder, and milk mixture. Beat until completely mixed, approximately 3 minutes.

4. Pour batter into the prepared pan and bake for 55 to 60 minutes, or until golden brown.

5. Remove from oven and cool for 15 minutes on wire rack, then turn out onto plate.

Susie's Banana Bread

4 very ripe bananas, mashed

1½ cups unbleached all-purpose flour

½ cup whole-wheat flour

1 cup sugar

¼ teaspoon salt

2 teaspoons baking soda

½ cup vegetable oil

3 tablespoons orange juice concentrate, thawed

½ cup nuts, chopped (optional)

This is absolutely the best of the best banana breads. I love the way the orange adds zip to the recipe.

1. Preheat oven to 350°F. Lightly butter a 9 x 5 x 3-inch loaf pan.

2. In a large bowl, add bananas, flours, sugar, salt, baking soda, oil, and orange juice concentrate. With a wooden spoon, mix until smooth, then fold in nuts.

3. Spoon out batter into prepared pan.

4. Bake 50 to 60 minutes or until toothpick inserted in center comes out clean.

5. Remove pan from oven and cool for 15 minutes on wire rack, then turn out onto plate.

Very Blueberry Bread

3 cups unbleached all-purpose flour plus 1 tablespoon (to coat blueberries)

1¼ cups sugar

1½ cups milk

2 tablespoons lemon juice

1 teaspoon baking powder

1 teaspoon baking soda

2 teaspoons grated lemon peel

1½ to 2 cups fresh blueberries (or frozen, not thawed)

If you love blueberries, this recipe is for you.

1. Preheat oven to 350°F. Lightly butter a 9 x 5 x 3-inch pan.

2. In a large bowl, with a wooden spoon, mix 3 cups flour, sugar, milk, lemon juice, baking powder, baking soda, and lemon peel until mixed well.

3. In a separate bowl or plastic bag toss in blueberries and coat with remaining 1 tablespoon of flour (this keeps blueberries from sinking to bottom); fold them into batter. (Batter will be lumpy.)

4. Spoon batter into prepared pan, spreading evenly. Bake for 50 to 55 minutes or until toothpick inserted in center comes out clean.

5. Remove pan to wire rack. Cool for 10 minutes. Turn out onto plate.

NOTE: For this recipe you can substitute mandarin oranges for blueberries and it comes out very tasty. This also freezes well for 1 month.

Easy Corn Bread

1 cup cornmeal

1¼ cups unbleached all-purpose flour

¼ cup sugar

1 tablespoon baking powder

½ teaspoon baking soda

1 tablespoon corn syrup

½ teaspoon salt

1¼ cups milk

2 tablespoons white vinegar

½ cup vegetable oil

Kids like this one. It's great for freezing—just take out a fresh corn bread whenever you want.

1. Preheat oven to 375°F. Lightly butter an 8 x 8-inch square pan.

2. In a large bowl, combine cornmeal, flour, sugar, baking powder, baking soda, corn syrup, salt, milk, vinegar, and oil. With a wooden spoon, stir just until mixed.

3. Pour out into prepared pan and bake for 20 to 25 minutes or until golden.

4. Remove pan to wire rack and cool 15 minutes in pan. Turn out onto plate.

Variation
You can add ½ cup drained canned corn.

Healthy Gingerbread

1 cup whole-wheat pastry flour

½ cup rye flour

½ cup unbleached all-purpose flour

¼ cup wheat germ

3 tablespoons sugar

2 tablespoons non-fat dry milk powder (optional)

1¼ teaspoons ginger

1¼ teaspoons ground cinnamon

¼ teaspoon ground cloves

1 cup buttermilk

½ cup apple juice concentrate, thawed

½ cup dark molasses

¼ cup vegetable oil

This gingerbread is great–tasting and good for you as a snack or anytime.

1. Preheat oven to 350°F. Lightly butter a 9 x 9-inch baking pan.

2. In a large bowl, with a wooden spoon, stir flours, wheat germ, sugar, dry milk powder (if used), ginger, cinnamon, and cloves. Mix until combined. Add buttermilk, apple juice concentrate, molasses, and vegetable oil. Mix until smooth.

3. Pour batter into prepared pan. Bake 30 to 40 minutes, or until brown.

4. Cool on wire rack 10 minutes before removing from pan.

NOTE: Freezes well.

Joyce's Health Bread

1 cup raisins

½ cup dates, pitted and chopped

½ cup water

¾ cup sugar

1 cup bran or bran cereal

1 cup quick rolled oats

1 cup whole-wheat flour

2 teaspoons baking soda

1½ cups buttermilk

1 cup nuts, chopped

My friend introduced me to this bread when she brought it to a picnic. We all loved it. It's moist and slightly heavy, like a date-nut bread. You can serve it with or without butter. It's great for a brunch.

1. In a I-quart-size pan, boil raisins and dates in water until water evaporates. Set aside.

2. Preheat oven to 350°F. Lightly butter a 9½ x 5½ x 3-inch loaf pan.

3. In a large bowl, with a wooden spoon, stir sugar, bran or cereal, oats, flour, and baking soda; add buttermilk, stir until thoroughly combined, fold in raisin-date mixture and nuts.

4. Spoon out batter into prepared pan. Bake for I hour or until toothpick inserted in center comes out clean.

5. Cool on wire rack for IO minutes before removing from pan.

Aunt Jane's Oatmeal Bread

1 cup quick rolled oats plus 2
teaspoons (to sprinkle on top of
each loaf)

½ cup molasses

1 (¼-ounce) package active dry
yeast

¼ cup warm water (to dissolve
yeast)

½ teaspoon salt

4 to 5 cups unbleached all-
purpose flour

This one is an old family recipe. It's pretty—and just that bit of oats sprinkled on the top makes it extra special. It tastes great. I always plan on freezing the second loaf, but we end up eating them both (this recipe freezes well).

1. Lightly butter and flour two 9 x 5 x 3-inch loaf pans, tapping out excess flour.

2. In a 1-quart pan, bring 1 pint water to a boil, add 1 cup oats, and remove from stove to cool until lukewarm. Then add molasses, stirring with a spoon to mix.

3. In a measuring cup, add yeast and warm water until yeast is dissolved, then add to oat mixture and with a spoon stir until well mixed.

4. Transfer to a large bowl. When this is spongy to the touch, add salt; add flour slowly, a cup at a time, mixing after each addition with your hands or a wooden spoon.

5. Turn dough out onto a lightly floured surface and knead for 10 minutes.

6. Put dough back in bowl, cover, and set aside in a warm area. Allow to rise until double in bulk (approximately 1½ to 2 hours).

7. Punch dough down, cut into 2 halves; knead each half separately into smooth balls and shape each ball into its own prepared pan. Cover pans with a cloth, allow to rise another 45 minutes in pans.

8. Preheat oven to 350°F.

9. Uncover pans. Make one long slice ¼ inch deep down the middle of each loaf and sprinkle 1 teaspoon of oats on top of each.

10. Place pans in the oven and bake for 40 to 50 minutes or until loaves look browned.

11. Cool on wire rack for 15 minutes before removing from pans.

Grandma's Irish Soda Bread

4 cups unbleached all-purpose
flour

2 tablespoons caraway seeds

¼ cup sugar

3 teaspoons baking powder

1½ teaspoons baking soda

½ teaspoon salt

¼ cup margarine or butter, room
temperature

1 cup raisins

1 tablespoon vegetable oil

1½ cups buttermilk

¼ cup club soda

Milk (to brush on top)

This family recipe is more than 100 years old. I've modified it slightly for this book, but the taste is still there. A great holiday traditional bread.

1. Preheat oven to 375°F. Lightly butter a 9-inch round baking pan or ovenproof casserole.

2. In a large bowl, with a wooden spoon, combine flour, caraway seeds, sugar, baking powder, baking soda, and salt; stir until mixed. With a pastry blender or your hands, work in the margarine or butter until moist; add raisins, then stir in oil, buttermilk, and club soda. Stir until moistened.

3. Scrape dough out onto a lightly floured board. Knead lightly until smooth.

4. Shape into a ball and place into prepared casserole pan.

5. With a sharp knife cut a 4-inch-long cross ¼ inch deep on top and brush with milk.

6. Bake for 45 to 55 minutes or until bread sounds hollow when tapped. Loosen sides with knife and lift out to tap bottom. Cool on wire rack 15 minutes. Then move to a plate.

NOTE: If you do not have club soda, just add ¼ cup more buttermilk.

Lemon Bread

makes 1 loaf

2½ cups unbleached all-purpose
  flour

1 cup sugar

2 teaspoons baking soda

3 teaspoons baking powder

1 tablespoon grated lemon peel

2 tablespoons lemon juice

½ cup sour cream

½ cup milk

Moist and delicious, this one is definitely for the lemon lover.

1. Preheat oven to 325°F. Lightly butter an 8½ x 4½ x 2½-inch ovenproof glass pan.

2. In a large bowl, with a wooden spoon, stir flour, sugar, baking soda, baking powder, lemon peel, lemon juice, sour cream, and milk.

3. Spoon out into prepared pan and bake for 30 to 40 minutes until toothpick inserted in center comes out clean.

4. Cool in pan on wire rack for 20 minutes before serving.

Orange Oat Bread

2 cups unbleached all-purpose
flour

1 cup quick rolled oats

1 cup sugar

2 teaspoons baking powder

1 teaspoon baking soda

½ stick butter or margarine,
melted

½ cup frozen orange juice
concentrate, thawed

2 tablespoons grated orange peel

¾ cup orange soda

1 cup chopped walnuts (optional)

This is a healthy snack. It is not too sweet, and it has the consistency of an old-fashioned gingerbread. Perfect as a bread or a cake, it goes well with just about anything including ice cream or cream cheese.

1. Preheat oven to 350°F. Lightly butter a 9 x 5 x 3-inch loaf pan.

2. In a large bowl, with a wooden spoon, mix flour, oats, sugar, baking powder, baking soda, butter or margarine, orange juice concentrate, orange peel, and orange soda. Stir quickly until dry ingredients are moistened. Stir in walnuts (if used).

3. Pour into prepared loaf pan. Bake for 35 to 45 minutes or until toothpick inserted in center comes out clean.

4. Cool on wire rack in pan for 10 minutes, then remove from pan and cool completely on wire rack.

Elegant Orange Raisin Bread

2 cups unbleached all-purpose
flour plus 1 tablespoon (to coat
raisins)

1½ teaspoons baking soda

1 cup sugar

½ cup frozen orange juice
concentrate, thawed

½ cup club soda

1 tablespoon grated orange peel

2 tablespoons butter, melted

2 tablespoons vegetable oil

¾ cup raisins

¾ cup walnuts, chopped

This orange bread is delicious and refined. It is great for a tea party.

1. Preheat oven to 350°F. Lightly butter a 9 x 5 x 3-inch loaf pan.

2. In a large bowl, combine 2 cups flour, baking soda, sugar, orange juice, club soda, orange peel, melted butter, and oil. With a wooden spoon, mix well. Toss raisins into a plastic bag with remaining 1 tablespoon flour and shake to coat (or they will sink to bottom). Fold raisins and nuts into batter.

3. Pour into prepared pan and bake for 40 to 50 minutes or until toothpick inserted in center comes out clean.

4. Cool completely on wire rack before slicing.

Orange Cranberry Loaf

2 cups unbleached all-purpose
   flour

2 teaspoons baking powder

1 teaspoon baking soda

1¼ cups sugar

2 tablespoons quick rolled oats

2 tablespoons vegetable oil

¾ cup frozen orange juice
   concentrate, thawed

⅓ cup plain low-fat yogurt

1 cup whole fresh cranberries,
   rinsed and chopped (or frozen,
   not thawed)

1 cup walnuts, chopped

This bread is great anytime, and is especially festive at holiday time.

1. Preheat oven to 350°F. Lightly butter and flour a 9 x 5 x 3-inch loaf pan, tapping out excess flour.

2. In a large bowl, with a wooden spoon, stir flour, baking powder, baking soda, sugar, quick oats, oil, orange concentrate, and yogurt until well mixed; fold in cranberries and nuts (batter will be thick).

3. Pour batter into prepared pan and bake for 40 to 50 minutes or until toothpick inserted in center comes out clean.

4. Cool completely on wire rack before slicing.

Kathleen's Pumpkin Bread

2¼ cups unbleached all-purpose
    flour

1⅓ cups sugar

2 teaspoons baking powder

1 teaspoon baking soda

1 teaspoon ground cinnamon

½ teaspoon ground nutmeg

1 cup canned plain pumpkin
    filling

1 teaspoon vanilla extract

¼ cup vegetable oil

½ cup buttermilk

1 cup raisins

1 cup nuts, chopped (optional)
    (your choice of nuts)

This healthy bread tastes wonderful any time of the year. It is nice and moist. I use raw walnuts since my daughter is able to have them.

1. Preheat oven to 350°F. Lightly butter a 9 x 5 x 3-inch loaf pan.

2. In a large bowl, combine flour, sugar, baking powder, baking soda, cinnamon, and nutmeg; with a wooden spoon, mix slowly. Add pumpkin, vanilla, oil, and buttermilk one at a time; stir until well combined. Fold in raisins and nuts.

3. Pour into prepared pan and bake for 40 to 50 minutes until golden brown or until toothpick inserted in center comes out clean.

4. Remove from oven onto wire rack and cool 10 minutes in pan. Turn out onto plate.

Tropical Island Bread

BREAD

5½ cups unbleached all-purpose flour, divided

2 (¼-ounce) packages active dry yeast

1 cup warm water

2 teaspoons granulated sugar

3 tablespoons vegetable oil

1 cup banana baby food or mashed banana

⅔ cup undiluted pineapple-orange-banana juice concentrate, thawed

¼ cup plus 1 teaspoon honey

½ teaspoon salt

Vegetable oil cooking spray

TOPPING

⅓ cup cream of coconut

2 tablespoons undiluted pineapple-orange-banana juice concentrate, thawed

⅓ cup sifted powdered sugar

3 tablespoons coconut (to sprinkle on top)

1 teaspoon colored sprinkles (to sprinkle on top)

This bread has a great fruity flavor. Serve on a special occasion and be sure to try this one at brunch, where it is sure to brighten your table.

1. *TO PREPARE BREAD:* In a medium bowl, measure the flour into the bowl with a correct-size dry measuring cup, scraping off top with a butter knife. Set aside.

2. In a separate measuring cup, dissolve yeast, water, and sugar; let stand 5 minutes. Then add oil, banana, juice concentrate, honey, and salt.

3. In a large bowl, combine yeast mixture slowly with 1 cup of flour at a time, mixing with a wooden spoon after each addition until dough is smooth.

4. Turn dough out onto a floured surface; knead until it is smooth (approximately 10 minutes), adding small amounts of extra flour if needed so it does not stick to your hands.

5. Coat the large bowl with vegetable oil spray. Put the dough back in the bowl and also lightly spray the top (just to completely coat).

6. In a warm place, cover for 1½ to 2 hours until double in size. Punch dough down; turn onto floured surface. Cut off 2-inch pieces and shape into balls by rolling with your hands; spray a 12-cup Bundt pan with vegetable oil and layer pan with balls of dough evenly. Cover the pan, set aside, and let rise another 45 minutes.

7. Preheat oven to 350°F. Uncover the pan and bake for 30 to 40 minutes or until golden brown.

8. Let cool in pan for 30 minutes, then turn out onto wire rack.

9. *TO PREPARE TOPPING:* In a small bowl, with a spoon, mix cream of coconut, juice concentrate, powdered sugar (add a little more confectioners' sugar for a thicker consistency if desired).

10. Drizzle over the cake, sprinkle with coconut and colored sprinkles.

Variation

You may also top with pineapple rings using 1 small can of drained pineapple.

Sesame Bread

3 cups unbleached all-purpose
 flour

⅔ cup sugar

1 tablespoon baking powder

1 teaspoon baking soda

½ teaspoon salt

¾ cup walnuts, chopped

½ cup raisins

1½ tablespoons grated orange
 peel

1 cup orange juice

½ cup water

1 cup tahini (sesame paste),
 available in supermarkets or
 health food stores

4 tablespoons sesame seeds (to
 sprinkle on top)

This is a sweet bread, more like a dessert. It is good with meals or a brunch.

1. Preheat oven to 350°F. Lightly butter and dust with flour a 9 x 13-inch pan, tapping out excess flour.

2. In a large bowl, sift flour, and add sugar, baking powder, baking soda, salt, walnuts, raisins, and orange peel. With a wooden spoon, stir until combined.

3. In a small bowl, with a wooden spoon, mix orange juice, water, and the sesame paste. Blend thoroughly and carefully (it will be very thick). Pour into flour mixture and mix well.

4. Spoon into pan and spread evenly. Sprinkle top with sesame seeds. Bake for 45 minutes or until top of bread springs back when touched with your finger.

5. Remove from oven and cool in pan on wire rack.

Walnut Bread

2½ cups unbleached all-purpose
  flour
1 tablespoon baking powder
½ teaspoon baking soda
¼ cup butter, room temperature
¾ cup firmly packed dark brown
  sugar
2 tablespoons vegetable oil
¾ cup buttermilk
1½ teaspoons vanilla extract
1 cup walnuts, chopped

A friend of mine makes this bread often because she and her family love the taste. Like them, you may well get hooked on the great flavor.

1. Preheat oven to 350°F. Lightly butter an 8½ x 4½ x 2½-inch loaf pan.

2. In a medium bowl, sift flour, baking powder, and baking soda. Set aside.

3. In a large bowl, with a wooden spoon, cream butter and sugar; add oil, buttermilk, and vanilla. Slowly add the flour mixture a little at a time, stirring after each addition until thoroughly mixed. Fold in nuts.

4. Pour batter into prepared pan. Bake for 50 to 60 minutes or until wooden toothpick inserted in center comes out clean.

5. Cool in pan for 10 minutes on wire rack. Then remove from pan and cool completely on wire rack.

Cinchy Whole-Wheat Buttermilk Soda Bread

makes 1 loaf

2 cups whole-wheat flour

½ cup sugar

2 cups buttermilk

2½ teaspoons baking soda

1 teaspoon quick rolled oats (to sprinkle on top)

This one is simple to make. You can double the recipe to make 2 loaves. They'll go fast!

1. Preheat oven to 350°F. Lightly butter an 8½ x 4½ x 2½-inch loaf pan.

2. In a large bowl, combine flour and sugar. Slowly add buttermilk and baking soda. With a wooden spoon, stir until mixed.

3. Pour batter into prepared pan, sprinkle oats on top, and bake for 1 hour or until cake tester comes out clean.

4. Cool completely for 10 minutes on wire rack and remove from pan.

Zucchini Bread

3 cups unbleached all-purpose
  flour

1½ cups sugar

2 teaspoons baking soda

3 teaspoons double-acting baking
  powder

1½ teaspoons ground cinnamon

¾ cup apple juice

1 teaspoon vanilla extract

1 cup chopped nuts

2 cups grated fresh zucchini

This zucchini bread is a must-try. It is moist and delicious without the fat (unless you add the nuts—of course I always use walnuts).

1. Preheat oven to 350°F. Lightly oil bottom of a non-stick 9 x 5-inch loaf pan.

2. In a large bowl, with a wooden spoon, combine flour, sugar, baking soda, baking powder, and cinnamon.

3. Add apple juice, vanilla, and chopped nuts to grated zucchini; then fold into batter until completely mixed.

4. Pour batter into prepared pan. Bake for 40 to 50 minutes until golden brown.

5. Remove from oven and cool completely on wire rack.

Brown Breadsticks

2 cups yellow cornmeal

2 cups warm water

½ cup firmly packed brown sugar

¼ cup light molasses

2 tablespoons vegetable oil

1 (¼-ounce) package dry yeast

1¾ cups whole-wheat flour

1½ cups rye flour

1 teaspoon salt

2 cups unbleached all-purpose
flour

Vegetable oil cooking spray

3 tablespoons caraway seeds

These are great with any meal, and are a must-serve at Thanksgiving.

1. Sprinkle ½ cup of cornmeal on 2 large baking sheets, reserving remaining 1½ cups. Set aside.

2. In a small bowl, combine water, sugar, molasses, oil, and yeast; stir to dissolve. Let stand until foamy.

3. In a large bowl, combine remaining 1½ cups of cornmeal, whole-wheat flour, rye flour, and salt. Add yeast mixture and stir with a wooden spoon; add ½ cup at a time of all-purpose flour and mix until dough is smooth. Turn out onto a lightly floured surface and knead until dough is smooth and elastic (approximately 15 minutes), adding more flour if necessary. Spray bowl with vegetable spray to coat and transfer dough back in bowl; spray top with vegetable spray just to coat, cover with towel, and let rise until double in size, approximately 1½ hours.

4. Punch down dough and turn out onto lightly floured work surface. Roll dough out approximately 8 inches long and 2 inches wide so you can cut 20 strips.

5. Roll each strip to 12-inch-long ropes. Cut them in half and twist each one into a 6 x 1-inch piece. Lightly spray tops with vegetable oil; sprinkle each with caraway seeds. Transfer them to prepared baking sheets. Space 3 inches apart. Place in a warm draft-free area for approximately another half-hour to rise.

6. Preheat oven to 425°F. Uncover the baking sheets and bake for 15 to 20 minutes or until outsides are crisp.

7. Completely cool 10 minutes on wire rack before removing from baking sheets.

Puffy Baking Powder Biscuits

2 cups unbleached all-purpose
flour

2 teaspoons baking powder

½ teaspoon salt

⅓ cup margarine or butter, room
temperature, plus 1 tablespoon
if needed

¾ cup buttermilk

Get ready, these biscuits taste great and they really puff up!

1. In a large bowl, with a pastry blender, mix flour, baking powder, salt, and margarine or butter until dough resembles crumbly
mixture. Slowly add buttermilk until a dough is formed (add a tablespoon more of margarine if dough does not hold together).
Turn out onto floured surface and knead dough for 50 seconds or
until it holds together.

2. Preheat oven to 400°F. Lightly butter a cookie sheet.

3. Pinch off twelve 1-inch pieces of dough and with your hands
roll a 1-inch golf-ball size. Place 2 inches apart on prepared
cookie sheet and press down with the bottom rim of a glass to flatten.

4. Bake 10 minutes or until brown.

5. Completely cool on wire rack.

Beer Biscuits

1¼ cups unbleached all-purpose
   flour

2 teaspoons baking powder

1 teaspoon baking soda

2 tablespoons milk

4 ounces light beer

1½ tablespoons sugar

2 tablespoons butter, room
   temperature

If you are a beer lover, these are great—that beer flavor really comes through. Serve with dinner.

1. Preheat oven to 400°F. Lightly butter six 3 x 1¼-inch (3½ to 4-ounce) muffin cups.

2. In a medium bowl, with a wooden spoon, mix flour, baking powder, baking soda, milk, beer, sugar, and butter until combined.

3. Cover bowl with towel and let stand for 15 minutes to rise. Spoon batter into prepared muffin tins and bake for 10 to 15 minutes until brown.

Oat Bran Biscuits

1 cup bran or bran cereal

¾ cup buttermilk

1¾ cups unbleached all-purpose
   flour

¼ cup quick rolled oats

3 tablespoons sugar

2 teaspoons baking powder

1 teaspoon baking soda

¼ cup butter or margarine, room
   temperature

These are great as a healthy breakfast or snack.

1. Preheat oven to 400°F. Lightly butter 2 large cookie sheets.

2. In a large bowl, combine bran and buttermilk. Set aside approximately 5 minutes. Then, with a wooden spoon, stir in flour, oats, sugar, baking powder, baking soda, and butter or margarine until it resembles a sticky dough. Cut dough in half and work with half at a time. Place half of dough on a floured surface and pat it out flat with your hands, then use a floured rolling pin and roll out dough to ½-inch thickness.

3. With a floured 2-inch cookie cutter or floured glass, cut into round shapes and transfer to prepared cookie sheets spacing 1 inch apart. Repeat for second half of dough and roll out remaining scraps until dough is all used up. Transfer them to cookie sheets and bake for 10 to 15 minutes until golden.

4. Cool on wire rack.

Dinner Biscuits

1 (¼-ounce) package dry yeast

¾ cup warm water

¼ cup sugar

2 tablespoons applesauce

1 teaspoon baking soda

½ cup evaporated milk

3¾ cups sifted unbleached all-
purpose flour

Vegetable oil cooking spray

These biscuits are like small round breads, each with a nice crust and truly delicious.

1. In a large bowl, dissolve yeast in warm water and sugar. Let stand for 3 minutes; add applesauce, baking soda, and evaporated milk. With a wooden spoon, slowly stir in 2 cups flour, beat until smooth, and work in remaining flour a little at a time, kneading to form a smooth dough. Cover dough with a damp towel and refrigerate overnight.

2. Preheat oven to 375°F. Spray 2 cookie sheets with vegetable oil cooking spray to coat pan.

3. Take dough out of refrigerator, let sit at room temperature for 5 minutes, and turn out onto a lightly floured work surface. With a lightly floured rolling pin, roll out dough to ¼-inch thickness. Cut dough with a floured 2-inch round glass or round cookie cutter.

4. Transfer rounds onto cookie sheets and bake 10 to 15 minutes or until golden brown.

5. Cool on wire rack for 5 minutes.

Crescents

1 (¼-ounce) package active dry
  yeast

½ cup warm water

2 tablespoons sugar

⅓ cup vegetable shortening

½ teaspoon salt

1 cup warm milk

3 to 4 cups sifted unbleached all-
  purpose flour

These are delicious served right out of the oven on a cold day, with butter.

1. In a small bowl, dissolve yeast in warm water and sugar. Set aside for a few minutes.

2. In a large bowl, with a fork, cream sugar, shortening, and salt; add milk and yeast mixture together. Slowly add flour ½ cup at a time, mixing after each addition.

3. Mold into a round ball (dough will be hard to handle) in bowl, and cover with damp towel. Place in a draft-free, warm area and let rise until double in size, approximately 1 hour. Turn dough out onto floured surface and with rolling pin roll into a circle like a pizza ¼ inch in thickness. Cut circle into 12 wedges like a pizza.

4. Lightly butter 2 large cookie sheets.

5. Roll up each wedge beginning at large end to the point and curve the ends. Transfer to 2 prepared cookie sheets.

6. Cover with a towel. Let rise on the cookie sheets another 45 minutes.

7. Meanwhile, preheat oven to 425°F.

8. Remove towel and bake in oven 10 to 15 minutes, until light brown.

Mom's Easter Bread (Taralli) With Anise Seeds

¼ cup warm water plus 1
  teaspoon sugar

2 (¼-ounce) packages active dry
  yeast

2½ cups warm milk plus 2
  teaspoons milk (to brush tops)

2 tablespoons lemon juice or
  white vinegar

6 cups unbleached all-purpose
  flour

1 cup sugar

1 tablespoon grated lemon zest or
  vanilla extract

3 tablespoons baking powder

¼ cup vegetable shortening or
  butter

¼ teaspoon salt

2½ teaspoons anise seeds

1 teaspoon candy sprinkles (to
  sprinkle on top)

This is my family's traditional holiday bread. Of course, you needn't be Italian to serve it, and don't wait until Easter!

1. In a small measuring cup, combine warm water mixture and yeast to dissolve. Set aside.

2. In a 1-quart pan, heat 2½ cups milk just until warm; add lemon juice or white vinegar. Set aside.

3. Meanwhile, in a large bowl, combine flour, 1 cup sugar, salt and anise seeds, lemon zest or vanilla, baking powder, and shortening or butter. Slowly add milk mixture (adding a little more milk if necessary) until it resembles a slightly sticky dough. Turn out onto floured surface and knead for 15 minutes until smooth. Return dough to bowl, cover with cloth, and place in a warm, draft-free area for approximately 3½ to 4 hours to rise.

4. Flour a large cookie sheet.

5. With a sharp knife, cut a long 3-inch in diameter piece from the ball of dough. On a lightly floured surface, roll into 10 x 2-inch log with your hands until smooth; repeat and make 2 more logs. Braid the 3 logs together to make 1 loaf.

6. Transfer loaf to prepared cookie sheet; repeat step 5 to make another loaf, spacing loaves 5 inches apart on the baking sheet. Cover with cloth and allow to rise on cookie sheet again for 1 hour or until double in bulk.

7. Preheat oven to 375°F. Uncover loaves. Brush tops with a little milk and sprinkle with candy sprinkles. Bake for 30 minutes or until bottom is hollow sounding when bread is removed and tapped.

8. Cool 10 minutes on wire rack before removing from pan.

Fun, Soft Pretzels

makes 3 to 4 dozen pretzels, depending on shapes and sizes

1 (¼-ounce) package active dry yeast

⅛ cup hot water

1¼ cups warm water

¼ cup firmly packed brown sugar

4½ cups unbleached all-purpose flour

Vegetable oil cooking spray

Baking soda

Salt

A large batch of New York–style pretzels that taste wonderfully fresh. Children love to help make these, and they certainly love eating them.

1. In a large bowl, dissolve yeast in hot water. Stir in warm water and sugar until mixed. Slowly add 1 cup at a time of flour, mixing after each addition. Mix until dough no longer sticks to sides of bowl.

2. Flour your hands and knead for 5 to 10 minutes until dough is smooth, adding a little more flour if dough is too sticky. Set aside.

3. Meanwhile, preheat oven to 475°F. Spray 2 cookie sheets with vegetable oil spray and set aside.

4. With a knife, cut a piece of dough a little bit larger than a golf ball; roll with your hands and shape into a pretzel.

5. Fill a large skillet or wok with water, adding 1 tablespoon of baking soda to every cup of water you add. Bring to a low boil on medium heat.

6. Place 4 pretzels at a time into the skillet for 40 to 50 seconds, then remove onto the prepared cookie sheets, spacing 1 inch apart. Sprinkle each pretzel with a little salt.

7. Place the sheets in the oven and bake for 8 minutes or until pretzels are golden brown.

Cakes

Miss Pat's Apple Cake

6 apples, peeled, cored, and chopped

2 cups plus ¼ cup sugar

5 teaspoons ground cinnamon

3½ cups unbleached all-purpose flour

4 teaspoons baking powder

1 cup vegetable oil

1 cup sour cream or yogurt

¾ cup orange juice

2 tablespoons vanilla extract

Loaded with apples and cinnamon, this apple cake is really a winner.

1. Preheat oven to 375°F. Lightly butter a 12-cup Bundt pan.

2. In a large bowl, with a wooden spoon, combine apples, ¼ cup sugar, and cinnamon until apples are completely coated; set aside.

3. In a separate large bowl, combine flour, remaining 2 cups sugar, and baking powder; make a well in center with a wooden spoon and stir in oil, sour cream or yogurt, orange juice, and vanilla. Mix until well blended (batter will be thick).

4. *TO ASSEMBLE CAKE:* Spoon out one third of batter into prepared Bundt pan, spoon out half of apple mixture (drained of excess moisture) around ring, being careful not to touch sides of pan with apples. Spoon out another third of batter over apple layer. Spoon out remaining apple mixture in same fashion and top with remaining batter.

5. Place in oven and bake for 45 minutes, then remove from oven and cover top with aluminum foil (so it does not over-brown). Return to oven for another 20 to 25 minutes or until toothpick inserted in center comes out clean.

6. Remove and cool in pan on wire rack for 20 minutes before turning onto plate.

NOTE: You can add ½ cup nuts to top and they bake right in.

Karen's Favorite Apple Cake

3 cups unbleached all-purpose
  flour

2 cups sugar

2 teaspoons baking soda

2 teaspoons vanilla extract

1¼ cups vegetable oil

½ cup buttermilk

1 teaspoon white vinegar

3 Granny Smith apples, peeled,
  cored, and sliced (approximately
  4 cups)

½ cup raisins

½ cup nuts

I've gathered many wonderful apple cake recipes, and each one is special. This has slices of apple and is very moist.

1. Preheat oven 350°F. Lightly butter a 12-cup Bundt pan.

2. In a large bowl, with a wooden spoon, combine flour, sugar, and baking soda. Slowly stir in one at a time, mixing after each addition, vanilla, oil, buttermilk, and vinegar. Combine until completely blended. Fold in apples, raisins, and nuts.

3. Spoon out batter with spatula into prepared pan and bake for 55 to 65 minutes or until toothpick inserted in center comes out clean.

4. Remove from oven, cool in pan for 15 minutes, then turn onto plate.

My Favorite Apple Cake

½ cup vegetable oil

2 cups sugar

1 cup applesauce

2¾ cups unbleached all-purpose flour

1½ teaspoons baking soda

2½ teaspoons baking powder

2 teaspoons ground cinnamon

2 teaspoons vanilla extract

3 apples, peeled, cored, and chopped (approximately 4 cups)

This is absolutely my favorite apple cake. It is loaded with cinnamon and smells just like a pie in the oven.

1. Preheat oven to 350°F. Butter and lightly flour a 12-cup Bundt pan. Tap out excess flour.

2. In a large bowl, with a wooden spoon, stir in one at a time, oil, sugar, applesauce, flour, baking soda, baking powder, cinnamon, and vanilla; fold in apples 1 cup at a time until completely mixed. This batter will be very thick.

3. Spoon out batter into prepared pan, spreading evenly. Bake for 50 to 60 minutes or until browned on top and toothpick inserted in center comes out clean.

4. Remove from oven, cool in pan on wire rack for 15 minutes, then turn onto plate.

Variations

For a less moist cake use ¾ cup applesauce instead of 1 cup. You can also add ½ cup nuts and/or ½ cup raisins.

Aunt Marge's Apple Raisin Cake

3 cups unbleached all-purpose
  flour

2 cups sugar

½ cup quick rolled oats

1 cup light sour cream

¼ cup milk

¼ cup club soda

2½ teaspoons baking soda

1½ teaspoons ground cinnamon

¼ teaspoon ground nutmeg
  (optional)

⅛ teaspoon ground cloves

3 cups apples, peeled, cored, and
  chopped

1 cup seedless raisins

½ cup coarsely chopped walnuts
  or almonds

My aunt Marge always served this cake with whipped cream. It is a little lighter than an average apple cake and always a hit.

1. Preheat oven to 350°F. Butter and lightly dust with flour a 12-cup Bundt pan. Tap out excess flour.

2. In large bowl, with a handheld electric mixer set on low speed, beat flour, sugar, oats, sour cream, milk, club soda, baking soda, cinnamon, nutmeg, and cloves until combined (batter will be thick). Fold in apples with a wooden spoon, then fold in raisins and nuts.

3. Spoon out batter into prepared pan and bake for 50 to 55 minutes.

4. Cool in pan for 15 minutes, then turn out onto plate. Serve with whipped cream or vanilla ice cream.

Applesauce Carrot Cake

makes 16 to 20 servings

¼ cup firmly packed light brown sugar

1¼ cups lightly sweetened applesauce

¼ cup vegetable oil

3 tablespoons plain low-fat yogurt

1 cup whole-wheat flour

½ cup unbleached all-purpose flour

1 teaspoon ground cinnamon

2 teaspoons baking powder

1 teaspoon baking soda

1 cup rolled oats

1¼ cups firmly packed shredded carrots

TOPPING

1 (8-ounce) package low-fat cream cheese, room temperature

1½ tablespoons grated lemon rind

2 tablespoons orange juice concentrate, thawed

1¼ teaspoons vanilla extract

This cake is excellent with the cream cheese frosting or by itself. It is special enough for a king or queen.

1. Preheat oven to 350°F. Butter a 9-inch square pan.

2. In a large bowl, with a handheld electric mixer set on medium speed, beat for 3 minutes brown sugar, applesauce, oil, yogurt, both flours, cinnamon, baking powder, baking soda, and rolled oats until well mixed. With a wooden spoon, fold in carrots until combined.

3. Spoon out batter evenly into the prepared pan and bake 30 to 40 minutes. Cool before frosting.

4. *TO PREPARE TOPPING:* In a small bowl, with a handheld electric mixer set on medium speed, beat cream cheese until smooth, approximately 1 minute. Then add at once lemon rind, concentrate, and vanilla. Blend for 3 minutes until creamy. Spread over top of cake and enjoy!

Apricot cake

1 standard-size (1-pound, 2¼-
ounce) box yellow cake mix,
pudding included

⅓ cup unbleached all-purpose
flour

1 teaspoon baking powder

1 cup ginger ale or lemon soda

⅓ cup vegetable oil

1 teaspoon vanilla extract

1 (8-ounce) jar apricot with
tapioca baby food

FROSTING

1 cup apricot preserves

1 (8-ounce) package cream
cheese, room temperature

⅓ cup margarine or butter

2½ cups confectioners' sugar

½ cup chopped walnuts

FILLING

⅓ cup apricot preserves

This festive cake is perfect for a special occasion.

1. Preheat oven to 350°F. Lightly butter a 12-cup Bundt pan.

2. *TO PREPARE CAKE:* In a large bowl, combine cake mix, flour, baking powder, ginger ale or lemon soda, oil, vanilla, and baby food. Beat with a handheld electric mixer set on medium speed for 3 minutes or until completely smooth. Spoon out batter into prepared pan and bake for 30 to 40 minutes, until toothpick inserted in center comes out clean. Cool in pan for 15 minutes, then turn out onto plate.

3. *TO PREPARE FROSTING:* When cake has cooled, in a 1-quart pan over low heat, warm apricot preserves. Set aside. In a small bowl, with a handheld electric mixer set on medium speed, beat cream cheese and margarine or butter until smooth. Add confectioners' sugar and warm preserves (adding more preserves if necessary for consistency). Fold in walnuts. Set aside.

4. *TO ASSEMBLE CAKE:* When cake is completely cooled, cut the cake in the center and spread filling over the bottom half. Place the top half back on the cake evenly when done.

5. Frost the top and sides of the cake with the frosting.

Apricot Brunch Cake

½ cup graham cracker crumbs

½ cup butter or margarine, melted

3½ cups unbleached all-purpose flour

1 teaspoon baking soda

1 teaspoon pumpkin pie spice (optional)

¼ teaspoon ground cloves

½ cup firmly packed brown sugar

1 cup granulated sugar

1 (8-ounce) jar apricot in tapioca baby food

½ cup vegetable oil

2 tablespoons rum or ½ teaspoon rum extract

1 cup milk

1 tablespoon lemon juice

¾ cup raisins (optional)

½ cup nuts, chopped (your choice)

FILLING

1 (1-pound) can apricot halves in heavy syrup, drained

½ cup coconut (optional)

½ cup walnuts, chopped

GLAZE

1 cup powdered sugar

1 teaspoon margarine or butter

½ teaspoon rum

6 teaspoons milk

This cake and filling are unbelievably delicious. The combination of graham cracker, rum, and apricot makes this a definite must-try.

1. Preheat oven to 375°F. Lightly butter a 12-cup Bundt pan, then sprinkle with graham cracker crumbs and ½ cup melted butter or margarine.

2. In a large bowl, with a handheld electric mixer, beat in flour, baking soda, pumpkin pie spice, cloves, sugars, apricot baby food, oil, rum, milk, lemon juice, raisins (if used), and nuts; beat 3 minutes on medium speed until completely combined.

3. Pour half of batter over graham cracker crumbs in pan.

4. *TO ASSEMBLE FILLING:* Place apricot halves around center avoiding edges, then sprinkle coconut over apricots evenly, and sprinkle nuts evenly over coconut. Spoon out remaining batter evenly on top of filling. Bake for 35 to 40 minutes or until toothpick inserted in center comes out clean. Cool completely on wire rack.

5. *TO PREPARE GLAZE:* In small bowl, with a handheld electric mixer set on medium speed, beat powdered sugar, margarine, rum, and milk until drizzling consistency. Drizzle over cake.

Out-of-This-World Banana, Carrot, and Pineapple Cake

CAKE

3½ cups unbleached all-purpose flour

1 (3.8-ounce) package banana or vanilla pudding

1 (4-ounce) jar banana baby food

1¾ cups granulated sugar

3½ teaspoons baking powder

2 teaspoons baking soda

⅓ cup vegetable oil

1 cup tonic water or club soda

1 teaspoon ground cinnamon

1 cup shredded carrots

1 (6-ounce) can crushed pineapple with juice

½ cup walnuts or almonds, chopped

FROSTING

1 (8-ounce) package cream cheese, room temperature

2 cups confectioners' sugar

2 tablespoons milk

2 teaspoons vanilla extract

½ cup flaked coconut (optional)

Awesome, fantastic, out-of-this-world—that's the consensus among everyone who's tried this one.

1. Preheat oven to 350°F. Lightly butter and flour a 12-cup Bundt pan, tapping out excess flour.

2. In a large bowl, combine flour, pudding, baby food, sugar, baking powder, baking soda, oil, tonic water or club soda, cinnamon, shredded carrots, pineapple, and nuts. With a wooden spoon, mix until smooth and completely blended.

3. Pour into prepared pan with spatula. Bake for 40 to 50 minutes or until toothpick inserted in center comes out clean.

4. Cool 10 minutes on wire rack, then turn onto plate and cool completely.

5. *TO PREPARE FROSTING:* In a medium bowl, using a handheld electric mixer set at medium-high speed, beat cream cheese until creamy. With mixer set at low speed, gradually beat in sugar, and add milk and vanilla. Beat until smooth (adding a little more milk 1 tablespoon at a time if necessary). Fold in coconut (if used) with a spoon.

6. Frost top and sides of cake. Refrigerate until ready to serve.

Rose's No-Fail Banana Cake

2 cups unbleached all-purpose
flour

1 cup quick rolled oats

½ cup granulated sugar

¾ cup firmly packed brown sugar

2 teaspoons baking soda

2 tablespoons baking powder

2 tablespoons poppy seeds
(optional)

5 bananas (mashed)

1 teaspoon grated lemon peel

1 tablespoon vanilla extract

½ cup raisins (optional)

½ cup vegetable oil

⅓ cup orange juice or water

½ cup walnuts, chopped
(optional)

This cake is very easy, and still comes out great every time.

1. Preheat oven to 350°F. Lightly butter a 12-cup Bundt pan.

2. In a large bowl, combine flour, oats, sugars, baking soda, baking powder, and poppy seeds (if used). With a wooden spoon, stir in mashed bananas, lemon peel, vanilla, raisins (if used), oil, and orange juice or water until completely mixed. (If batter is too thick and you cannot get the spoon through it add a little more juice or water); fold in the nuts (if used) at the end.

3. Spoon out batter into prepared pan and bake for 40 to 50 minutes or until golden brown.

4. Cool in pan on wire rack.

Banana-Chocolate Cake

makes 12 servings

CAKE

1 (4-ounce) bar sweet cooking
  chocolate

¼ cup water

2½ cups unbleached all-purpose
  flour

1½ cups granulated sugar

2 teaspoons baking soda

¾ cup vegetable shortening

1 cup mashed ripe bananas

1½ teaspoons vanilla extract

1 cup buttermilk

¼ cup vegetable oil

1 cup pecans or walnuts, chopped

FILLING

¾ cup granulated sugar

¾ cup evaporated milk

3 tablespoons butter or
  margarine, room temperature

1 teaspoon cornstarch

3 tablespoons vegetable oil

¾ cup chopped nuts

¼ cup mashed ripe banana

1½ teaspoons vanilla extract

The banana-chocolate combination is a delightful surprise, making this a delicious cake.

1. *TO PREPARE CAKE:* Preheat oven to 375°F. Lightly butter three 8-inch round pans.

2. In a small saucepan over low heat, melt chocolate in double boiler. Or in a microwave-safe bowl with microwave set on high, melt chocolate for 1 minute. Stir in water. Set aside.

3. In a large bowl, combine flour, sugar, and baking soda; with a handheld electric mixer set on slow speed, beat in melted chocolate, shortening, bananas, vanilla, buttermilk, and oil, blending well after each addition until completely smooth. Fold in nuts with a spoon.

4. Pour out batter evenly in the 3 prepared pans. Bake for 20 to 25 minutes or until toothpick inserted in center comes out clean. Cool 10 minutes in pans.

5. *TO PREPARE FILLING:* In a medium saucepan, combine sugar, evaporated milk, butter or margarine, cornstarch, and oil; with a spoon, stir constantly until well mixed. Cook over medium heat 10 minutes until thick, stirring constantly; add in nuts, mashed banana, and vanilla. Cool until spreading consistency.

GLAZE

1 (1-ounce) square unsweetened
  chocolate

2 tablespoons butter or margarine

1 cup confectioners' sugar

1 teaspoon vanilla extract

4 tablespoons milk

¼ cup chopped nuts (optional)

6. *TO PREPARE GLAZE:* In a small saucepan over low heat, melt chocolate and butter or margarine, stirring until smooth. Or melt in microwave, in a medium-size, microwave-safe bowl, on high setting for 1 minute. Remove from microwave.

7. With a handheld electric mixer set on medium speed, beat in confectioners' sugar, vanilla, and enough milk to bring glaze to spreading consistency. Set aside.

8. *TO ASSEMBLE CAKE:* Place first layer on a plate; spread top with half the filling mixture. Place second layer on top of first layer and spread the remaining half of filling mixture on top. Top with third layer and spoon glaze over top, allowing it to run down sides of cake. Sprinkle top of cake with nuts (if desired).

My Favorite Blueberry Poppy Seed Cake

CAKE

⅔ cup granulated sugar

½ cup butter or margarine or applesauce, room temperature

2 teaspoons grated lemon peel

½ cup quick rolled oats

1½ cup unbleached all-purpose flour

2 tablespoons poppy seeds

2 teaspoons baking soda

½ cup no-fat sour cream

FILLING

2½ cups drained fresh/frozen blueberries

⅓ cup granulated sugar

2 teaspoons unbleached all-purpose flour

¼ teaspoon ground nutmeg

GLAZE

⅓ cup confectioners' sugar

2 teaspoons milk or water

This really is a pretty cake and it is delicious. It's perfect for a fancy brunch or party and as an everyday snack.

1. *TO PREPARE CAKE:* Preheat oven to 350°F. Lightly butter and dust with flour a 9-inch springform pan, including sides. Tap out excess flour.

2. In a large bowl, with a handheld electric mixer set on medium speed, beat sugar and butter or margarine or applesauce until creamy; add lemon peel and oats. Slowly sift in flour; add poppy seeds, baking soda, and sour cream, scraping sides of bowl with a spatula.

3. Spread batter over bottom and 1 inch up the sides of prepared pan, creating a gradual curve shape, like the rounded bottom of a bowl, with the sides ¼ inch thick. Set aside.

4. *TO PREPARE FILLING:* In a medium bowl, combine blueberries, sugar, flour, and nutmeg. Spoon out over batter and bake for 45 to 55 minutes or until crust on sides is golden brown. Cool completely on wire rack, then remove sides of pan and place on a serving platter.

5. *TO PREPARE GLAZE:* In a small bowl, with a wooden spoon, mix the confectioners' sugar and milk or water (adding a little more milk or water if necessary until mixture is of drizzling consistency). Drizzle over top of cake and serve.

T.D.'S Sour Cream Coffee Cake

CAKE

½ cup butter or margarine, room temperature

1½ cups granulated sugar

2¾ cups unbleached all-purpose flour

1 tablespoon vinegar

2 teaspoons baking powder

1 teaspoon baking soda

1 cup low-fat sour cream

2 teaspoons vanilla extract

¼ cup water

TOPPING AND FILLING

½ cup firmly packed brown sugar

1 cup finely chopped nuts

2 teaspoons ground cinnamon

2 tablespoons butter or margarine, melted

2 tablespoons unbleached all-purpose flour

This cake was originated by my friend Theresa, who is a great baker. She always knows the best cakes to serve, and this is absolutely one of them.

1. Preheat oven to 350°F. Lightly butter and dust with flour a 12-cup Bundt pan. Tap out excess flour.

2. *TO PREPARE CAKE:* In a large bowl, with a handheld electric mixer set on medium speed, beat in butter or margarine, and sugar until fluffy. Beat in, one at a time, flour, vinegar, baking powder, baking soda, sour cream, vanilla, and water. (Batter will be thick; if too thick add a little water.) Set aside.

3. *TO PREPARE TOPPING AND FILLING:* In a medium bowl, with a fork, mash brown sugar, nuts, cinnamon, butter or margarine, and flour until they make a crumbly mixture. Set aside.

4. Pour half of batter into prepared pan. Sprinkle half of topping on batter. Pour rest of batter over topping and cover with remaining topping. Bake for 45 minutes or until toothpick inserted in center comes out clean. Cool on wire rack for 20 minutes, then invert onto a plate.

Loaded Blueberry UpSide Down Cake

CAKE

¾ cup vegetable shortening

2½ cups granulated sugar

4½ cups unbleached all-purpose flour plus 1 tablespoon (to coat blueberries)

2 teaspoons baking powder

1 (¼-ounce) package yeast

2½ cups warm milk

2 teaspoons lemon extract

¼ cup lemon juice

½ teaspoon grated lemon peel

1 (12-ounce) package frozen blueberries

CRUMB TOPPING (OPTIONAL)

¼ cup butter or margarine, room temperature

½ cup granulated sugar

⅓ cup unbleached all-purpose flour

½ teaspoon ground cinnamon

GLAZE

½ cup confectioners' sugar

¼ teaspoon vanilla extract

2 teaspoons hot water

This is a great cake any time—at breakfast, served at a buffet, or with a cup of tea. It is very moist and full of blueberries.

1. Preheat oven to 350°F. Butter a 10 x 13 x 2-inch non-stick pan.

2. In a large bowl, with a handheld electric mixer set on medium speed, cream shortening and sugar until fluffy. Change to low speed and slowly blend in 4½ cups flour and baking powder. Set aside.

3. In a measuring cup, add yeast to warmed milk to dissolve; set aside for 1 minute. Then add to flour mixture, scraping sides of bowl with a spatula; add extract, lemon juice, and lemon peel and mix until batter is smooth.

4. In a plastic bag or bowl, toss blueberries with remaining tablespoon flour and shake or gently stir until well coated. Fold berries into batter gently with a wooden spoon.

5. Pour into prepared cake pan. Set aside.

6. *TO PREPARE TOPPING (THIS IS OPTIONAL, IT WILL END UP ON THE BOTTOM):* In a medium bowl, with a pastry blender, combine all topping ingredients and blend until they make a crumbly mix. Sprinkle over top of cake and bake for 45 to 55 minutes or until toothpick inserted in center comes out clean. Cool completely in pan for 20 minutes, then turn out upside down onto rectangular serving tray.

7. *TO PREPARE GLAZE:* In a small bowl, combine confectioners' sugar, vanilla, and hot water. Stir with a spoon until glaze consistency. Spoon over cake after it is completely cooled.

1 standard-size (1-pound, 2¼-
  ounce) lemon cake mix,
  pudding included

8 ounces yogurt or sour cream

¼ cup vegetable oil

2 teaspoons baking powder

1 (12-ounce) package frozen
  blueberries

2 tablespoons flour

Confectioners' sugar (to sprinkle
  on top)

Variation

1. Preheat oven to 350°F. Lightly butter a 10-inch tube pan.

2. In a large bowl, blend cake mix, yogurt or sour cream, oil, and baking powder. With a handheld electric mixer set on medium speed, beat for 3 minutes. In a bowl or plastic bag, toss blueberries in 2 tablespoons of flour to coat. Fold into the batter just until mixed.

3. Pour batter into prepared pan and bake for 35 to 45 minutes or until toothpick inserted in center comes out clean. Cool 15 minutes in pan on wire rack, then remove. Sprinkle with confectioners' sugar.

Rose's Own Easy Carrot Spice Cake

2 cups firmly packed shredded carrots

2½ cups unbleached all-purpose flour

½ cup sugar (optional)

3 teaspoons baking powder

1 teaspoon baking soda

½ cup applesauce

1 (6-ounce) can frozen apple juice concentrate, thawed

¼ cup water

1 teaspoon vanilla extract

2 teaspoons ground cinnamon

½ cup flaked coconut (optional)

½ cup chopped walnuts (optional)

½ cup raisins (optional)

This cake is very moist and delicious and has no sugar. (If you want you can add it.)

1. Preheat oven to 350°F. Lightly butter a 12-cup Bundt pan.

2. To a large bowl, add carrots, and with a wooden spoon, stir in slowly flour, sugar (if used), baking powder, baking soda, applesauce, apple juice concentrate, water, vanilla, cinnamon, and coconut (if used). Fold in the nuts (if used) and raisins (if used) until completely mixed (if the batter is too thick and you cannot get a spoon through it, add more water).

3. Pour into prepared pan and bake for 40 to 50 minutes or until a toothpick inserted in center comes out clean.

4. Cool in pan on rack for 15 minutes and turn out onto a serving plate.

Variation

Replace carrots with grated sweet potato, substitute orange juice for apple juice, and add 1 extra teaspoon baking powder (this may need to cook a little longer).

Cola Cake

CAKE

½ cup butter or margarine, room temperature

1½ cups granulated sugar

3 tablespoons cocoa powder

2½ cups unbleached all-purpose flour

1 teaspoon baking soda

1 teaspoon baking powder

¾ cup buttermilk

2 teaspoons vanilla extract

1¼ cups cola soda

1½ cups mini-marshmallows (optional)

1 (3⅝-ounce) package instant chocolate pudding filling

FROSTING

¾ cup vegetable shortening

⅓ cup cola soda

½ teaspoon vanilla extract

1 pound confectioners' sugar

1 tablespoon cocoa powder

This cake is absolutely a favorite because of the great-tasting cola-chocolate combination. Kids especially love it with the tiny marshmallows included. It is guaranteed to be the topic of conversation at your party.

1. Preheat oven to 350°F. Lightly butter a 9 x 13-inch pan.

2. In a large bowl, with a handheld electric mixer set on medium speed, cream butter or margarine and sugar until fluffy. Slowly add one at a time cocoa, flour, baking soda, baking powder, buttermilk, vanilla, cola, marshmallows (if used), and chocolate pudding, mixing after each addition until completely blended.

3. Pour batter out into prepared pan and bake for 40 to 45 minutes or until toothpick inserted in center comes out clean. Cool in pan on wire rack for 10 minutes and turn out onto plate.

4. *TO PREPARE FROSTING:* In a large bowl, with a handheld electric mixer set on medium speed, beat vegetable shortening, cola, and vanilla. Stop mixer. Slowly add confectioners' sugar and cocoa a little at a time and continue to beat until completely creamy (add a little more cola and confectioners' sugar if not smooth enough). Frost the top and sides and serve.

christmas coffee cake

CAKE

2 cups unbleached all-purpose
   flour

1⅓ cups granulated sugar

½ cup (1 stick) low-fat butter,
   room temperature

1 cup light sour cream

2 teaspoons grated lemon peel

1 teaspoon lemon juice

½ cup vegetable oil

2 teaspoons vanilla extract

½ teaspoon lemon extract

2 teaspoons baking powder

1 teaspoon baking soda

FILLING

1 cup coarsely chopped walnuts

¼ cup firmly packed light brown
   sugar

1½ teaspoons ground cinnamon

2 tablespoons margarine, melted

TOPPING

2 teaspoons confectioners' sugar

This cake is a must on Christmas morning or at any special brunch. It is truly delicious.

1. Preheat oven to 350°F. Lightly butter and dust with flour a non-stick 12-cup Bundt pan. Tap out excess flour.

2. *TO PREPARE CAKE:* In a large bowl, sift in flour and sugar; with a handheld electric mixer set on medium speed, beat until smooth butter, sour cream, lemon peel, lemon juice, oil, vanilla and lemon extracts, baking powder, and baking soda. Set aside.

3. *TO PREPARE FILLING:* In medium-size bowl, mix walnuts, brown sugar, cinnamon, and melted margarine. Set aside.

4. *TO ASSEMBLE CAKE:* Spoon out two-thirds of batter into prepared pan; spread evenly with a rubber spatula. Sprinkle filling mixture over top evenly. Pour out remaining batter into pan evenly. Place on center rack of preheated oven and bake 35 to 45 minutes or until cake tester inserted near center comes out clean. Cool in pan on wire rack for 15 minutes, then turn out onto a serving plate and cool completely.

5. *TO PREPARE TOPPING:* When cooled, dust top with confectioners' sugar.

Bunnie's Mystery Spice Cake

2 cups unbleached all-purpose
   flour

1 cup sugar

1¼ teaspoons baking soda

1 teaspoon baking powder

½ teaspoon ground cloves

½ teaspoon ground nutmeg

1 teaspoon ground cinnamon

1 tablespoon vegetable oil

1 (10¾-ounce) can condensed
   tomato soup

½ can water

1 cup raisins

¼ cup nuts

This recipe originated from my friend Bunnie's mother and dates back to at least the Depression. Bunnie's philosophy is to keep the tomato soup a secret until after your guests ask for the recipe (and they will ask).

1. Preheat oven to 350°F. Lightly butter a 10-cup tube pan.

2. In a large bowl, with a wooden spoon, combine until mixed flour, sugar, baking soda, baking powder, cloves, nutmeg, and cinnamon.

3. Add oil and mix until smooth; add tomato soup and water and mix well. Fold in raisins and nuts.

4. Pour into prepared pan and bake for 50 to 60 minutes or until toothpick inserted in center comes out clean. Cool in pan on wire rack for 15 minutes, then turn onto plate.

Sour Cream Ring Cake

1¾ cups unbleached all-purpose
  flour

½ cup quick rolled oats

¾ cup granulated sugar

½ cup firmly packed brown sugar

¼ cup margarine or butter, room
  temperature

½ cup skim milk

1 cup low-fat sour cream

2 teaspoons baking soda

2 teaspoons baking powder

2 tablespoons lemon juice

2 teaspoons vanilla extract

½ cup chopped walnuts or
  almonds

This is delicious at breakfast or brunch. This cake freezes well.

1. Preheat oven to 350°F. Generously butter a 6-cup tube pan or an ovenproof ring mold.

2. In a large bowl, sift flour, oats, and sugars. With a handheld electric mixer set on low speed, blend in margarine or butter, milk, and sour cream for 2 minutes. Beat in baking soda, baking powder, lemon juice, and vanilla for another 2 minutes until smooth. Fold in nuts until evenly mixed.

3. Spoon out into prepared pan. Bake for 30 to 40 minutes or until toothpick inserted in center comes out clean. Cool on wire rack 15 minutes; invert onto serving plate. Cool completely.

Aunt Sharon's Favorite Chocolate Cake

3¼ cups unbleached all-purpose
  flour

2½ cups sugar

¾ cup cocoa or 5 (1-ounce)
  squares chocolate, melted

2 teaspoons baking powder

⅔ cup vegetable oil

2 tablespoons white vinegar

2¼ cups cold water

2½ teaspoons vanilla extract

This is a great, easy, quick cake to make, and it also freezes well.

1. Preheat oven to 375°F. Lightly butter a 9 x 13-inch pan.

2. In a large bowl, add flour, sugar, cocoa, and baking powder. Make a well in the center and add oil, vinegar, water, and vanilla. With a wooden spoon, stir until smooth and well blended.

3. Pour into prepared pan and bake for 40 minutes or until toothpick inserted in center comes out clean. Completely cool in pan on wire rack.

Variation

For cupcakes, cut recipe in half. Fill each cup of a 12-cup muffin pan two-thirds full and bake for 20 minutes. Cool completely on wire rack.

Beth's Chocolate Applesauce Cake

makes 16 to 20 servings

1½ cups unbleached all-purpose
  flour

¾ cup granulated sugar

¼ cup cocoa powder

1 teaspoon baking soda

1 teaspoon vanilla extract

1 cup applesauce

½ cup club soda

⅓ cup vegetable oil

1 tablespoon vinegar

CHOCOLATE FROSTING

½ cup water

1½ teaspoons instant coffee
  granules

½ cup firmly packed brown sugar

2¼ tablespoons butter or
  margarine

2 ounces unsweetened chocolate

2 cups confectioners' sugar

2 teaspoons vanilla extract

½ cup almonds, chopped

This is a great cake to serve to guests. It has a great chocolate flavor, is fast and easy to make, and has a nice glaze with a coffee flavor. It also freezes well.

1. *TO PREPARE CAKE:* Preheat oven to 350°F. Lightly butter an 8 x 8-inch square pan.

2. In a large bowl, sift flour, sugar, cocoa, baking soda; add vanilla, applesauce, club soda, oil, and vinegar. With a wooden spoon, stir until well combined. Pour out into prepared pan and bake for 30 to 35 minutes until golden in color. Cool 10 minutes in pan on wire rack and invert onto serving platter.

3. *TO PREPARE FROSTING:* In a 1-quart saucepan, on medium-high heat, boil water and add instant coffee, sugar, butter or margarine, and unsweetened chocolate until melted. Remove from heat and allow to cool until warm. Beat in confectioners' sugar and vanilla; sprinkle with almonds. When cooled, spread over cake.

Chocolate Mousse Divine Filling and Frosting

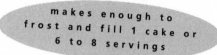

1 (¼-ounce) envelope unflavored
gelatin

3 tablespoons cold water

3 tablespoons boiling water

2 teaspoons vanilla extract

¼ cup granulated sugar

¼ cup confectioners' sugar

¼ cup cocoa powder

1 teaspoon instant coffee
granules (optional)

2 tablespoons brandy (optional)

1½ cups heavy cream (very cold)

Chocolate cookie crumbs
(optional)

Turn any cake in this book into a layer cake by doubling the recipe and using this for the filling and frosting. Or just scoop it out into servings and eat it as plain mousse.

1. In a small bowl, sprinkle gelatin over cold water; stir and let stand 3 minutes. Add boiling water; stir until gelatin is dissolved and cooled.

2. In a medium bowl, combine vanilla, sugars, cocoa, coffee granules (if used), and brandy (if used); stir with spoon. Add heavy cream, and with a handheld electric mixer set on medium speed, beat until stiff peaks form; then spoon in gelatin mixture and beat just to blend. Do not overbeat.

3. Cut in center and spread between layers and over top and sides of cake, and sprinkle top with crushed chocolate cookie crumbs if desired.

4. Chill about 1 hour before serving.

Variation

The chocolate mousse may be spooned out into small bowls and served as plain mousse; sprinkle with chocolate cookie crumbs.

Moist Rich-Tasting Chocolate Cake

CAKE

1½ cups water

2 teaspoons baking soda

2½ cups unbleached all-purpose
flour

2¼ cups granulated sugar

1¼ cups cocoa powder

2 teaspoons baking powder

½ cup light sour cream

¾ cup vegetable oil

2¼ teaspoons vanilla extract

FROSTING

3 cups chilled whipping cream
(very cold)

1½ cups confectioners' sugar

3½ tablespoons cocoa powder

2 teaspoons vanilla extract

½ cup chopped nuts (to sprinkle
on top)

This cake freezes well and is moist and rich tasting.

1. Preheat oven to 325°F. Lightly butter and dust with flour two 8 x 8-inch pans. Tap out excess flour.

2. In a 1-quart saucepan on medium-high heat, boil water and add baking soda, stirring until dissolved. Remove from heat and set aside.

3. In a large bowl, combine flour, sugar, cocoa, and baking powder. Then add baking soda/water mixture. With a handheld electric mixer set on medium speed, beat in the water and beat in one at a time sour cream, oil, and vanilla, stirring and scraping sides with a rubber spatula until completely mixed.

4. Pour batter into 2 prepared pans and bake for 40 to 50 minutes or until cake tester inserted in center comes out clean. Cool in pans for 15 minutes on wire rack and turn out onto plates; completely cool before frosting.

5. *TO PREPARE FROSTING:* In a large bowl, combine cream, sugar, cocoa, and vanilla. With a handheld electric mixer set on medium speed, whip until stiff peaks form.

6. Frost bottom half first, top with other cake, and frost sides and top of cake. Sprinkle top with nuts and chill 1 hour before serving.

Heavenly Chocolate Cake

makes 16 servings

CAKE

¾ cup cocoa powder

2½ cups unbleached all-purpose
flour

2½ teaspoons baking soda

1 cup butter or margarine, room
temperature

1 cup granulated sugar

2½ teaspoons vanilla extract

1 (3⅝-ounce) package instant
chocolate pudding filling

1¾ cups buttermilk

½ cup club soda

CREAMY TOPPING

¼ cup cocoa powder

1½ cups confectioners' sugar

½ cup milk

¼ cup butter

1 tablespoon corn syrup

1 teaspoon vanilla extract

½ cup chopped nuts

½ cup mini-marshmallows

This cake is absolutely heavenly. All good things come from heaven and that is why it is not called devil's food cake. This one is a must-try.

1. Preheat oven to 350°F. Lightly butter a 12-cup Bundt pan.

2. *TO PREPARE CAKE:* In a large bowl, combine cocoa, flour, baking soda, butter or margarine, granulated sugar, vanilla, chocolate pudding, buttermilk, and club soda. With a wooden spoon, stir vigorously until smooth.

3. Pour batter into prepared pan. Bake 35 to 45 minutes or until toothpick inserted in center comes out clean. Cool in pan on wire rack for 20 minutes, then turn out onto plate.

4. *TO PREPARE TOPPING:* In a 2-quart saucepan, stir together cocoa, confectioners' sugar, milk, butter, and corn syrup. Bring to a boil, stir vigorously for 2 minutes. Add vanilla and remove from burner; stir until mixture becomes thick. Spoon over cake, sprinkle with nuts and marshmallows, and serve.

Variation

May also be served with chocolate shavings and curls on top.

Vernice's Easiest Whole-Wheat Chocolate Cake

1¾ cups pure whole-wheat flour

1 cup granulated sugar

¼ cup cocoa powder

1 (3⅝-ounce) package instant chocolate pudding filling

1 teaspoon baking soda

2 teaspoons baking powder

¾ cup vegetable oil

1 teaspoon vanilla extract

1¼ cups warm water

1 teaspoon lemon juice

CARAMEL FROSTING

¾ cup firmly packed brown sugar

¼ cup granulated sugar

¼ cup milk

1½ tablespoons butter

2 teaspoons vanilla extract

1 teaspoon confectioners' sugar

This cake is for the health-conscious. It uses whole-wheat flour but it does not interfere with the chocolate flavor.

1. Preheat oven to 350°F.

2. In an ungreased 8 x 8 x 2-inch baking pan, combine flour, sugar, cocoa powder, chocolate pudding mix, baking soda, and baking powder. Pour in oil, vanilla, water, and lemon juice and, with a wooden spoon, stir until blended.

3. Place in oven on center rack and bake 35 to 45 minutes. Cool 15 minutes on wire rack and invert onto serving plate.

4. *TO PREPARE FROSTING:* In a 2-quart saucepan, over medium heat, combine sugars, milk, butter, and vanilla, stirring constantly until mixture boils and thickens. Remove from heat and whisk in confectioners' sugar, until frosting becomes thick enough to spread.

Chocolate Sour Cream Cake

makes 16 servings

1⅔ cups unbleached all-purpose
flour

1¼ cup granulated sugar

½ cup cocoa powder

1 teaspoon baking soda

1 cup sour cream or no-fat sour
cream

½ cup oil or apple juice

2 teaspoons vanilla extract

½ cup club soda

WHIPPED TOPPING

1 pint whipping cream

1 teaspoon instant coffee
granules

3 tablespoons confectioners'
sugar

2 tablespoons cocoa powder

½ cup walnuts, finely chopped

This cake is one of my favorites. It is moist and freezes well. The cake is easy to make and tastes rich and delicious.

1. Preheat oven to 350°F. Lightly butter a 9 x 13-inch pan.

2. In a large bowl, with a handheld electric mixer set on medium speed, beat flour, sugar, cocoa, baking soda, sour cream, oil or apple juice, vanilla, and club soda for 3 minutes or until completely mixed.

3. Pour into prepared pan and bake for 30 to 40 minutes. Cool completely in pan on wire rack; then invert onto a platter.

4. *TO PREPARE TOPPING:* In a small bowl, with a handheld electric mixer set on medium speed, whip cream until stiff peaks form, approximately 1 minute. Then beat in coffee granules, confectioners' sugar, and cocoa just until combined (do not overbeat). Spread over cake, sprinkle with nuts, and serve.

Perfect Chocolate Cupcakes

makes 12 cupcakes; will frost up to 24 cupcakes

CAKE BATTER

(See Chocolate Sour Cream Cake, page 63)

FROSTING

3 cups confectioners' sugar

½ cup cocoa powder

½ cup margarine, room temperature

1 teaspoon vanilla extract

¼ cup milk

This cupcake will also freeze well and the frosting is perfect!

1. Preheat oven to 350°F. Lightly butter 12-cup (4-ounce) muffin pan.

2. *TO PREPARE CAKE:* Prepare the previous recipe (Chocolate Sour Cream Cake).

3. In prepared pan, fill 12 muffin cups ¾ full. Bake for 15 to 20 minutes. Cool on wire rack approximately 20 minutes before removing from pan.

4. *TO PREPARE FROSTING:* Meanwhile, in a medium bowl, beat together confectioners' sugar, cocoa, margarine, vanilla, and milk with a handheld electric mixer set on medium speed for 3 minutes or until creamy. Frost cupcakes.

NOTE: Extra frosting will keep in refrigerator up to 2 weeks.

Heavenly Chocolate Mocha Cake

CAKE

2¼ cups unbleached all-purpose
  flour

1¾ cups granulated sugar

¾ cup cocoa powder

1¼ tablespoons baking soda

½ cup vegetable oil

1¼ cups buttermilk

1 cup strong coffee (instant can
  be used)

FUDGE TOPPING

3 tablespoons cocoa powder

1 cup granulated sugar

¼ cup evaporated skim milk

¼ cup margarine or butter

1 teaspoon vanilla extract

WHIPPED TOPPING

3 tablespoons confectioners'
  sugar

1 pint whipping cream

1 teaspoon instant coffee
  granules

1 tablespoon cocoa powder

1 teaspoon vanilla extract

This cake is absolutely heavenly. It is so moist and delicious you will be proud to serve it to your guests.

1. *TO PREPARE CAKE:* Preheat oven to 350°F. Lightly butter a 9 x 13-inch pan.

2. In a large bowl, sift together flour, sugar, cocoa, and baking soda. Add oil and buttermilk. With a wooden spoon, stir until completely mixed. Set aside.

3. Bring 1 cup of coffee to a complete boil, stir gently into batter, and mix (mixture will be soupy).

4. Pour into prepared pan and bake for 45 to 55 minutes. Cool completely on wire rack.

5. *TO PREPARE UNDERLAYER TOPPING:* In a 2-quart pan, combine cocoa, sugar, evaporated skim milk, margarine or butter, and vanilla. Over high heat, bring to a boil, remove from heat, and stir vigorously until thick enough to spread. Spread on cooled cake.

6. *TO PREPARE WHIPPED TOPPING:* In a medium bowl, combine confectioners' sugar, whipping cream, instant coffee granules, cocoa, and vanilla. With a handheld electric mixer set on medium speed, beat until creamy. Spread over the first underlayer of topping.

Mocha Cake With Almonds

½ cup chopped almonds

1⅓ cups strong coffee

½ cup margarine or butter

1 (12-ounce) package (2 cups) semisweet chocolate chips

½ cup plus 2 tablespoons granulated sugar

1 teaspoon almond extract

2 cups unbleached all-purpose flour

1½ teaspoons baking soda

2 teaspoons vanilla extract

2 tablespoons vinegar

Confectioners' sugar (to dust on top)

This cake has a delicious mocha taste. It is so good by itself, I never frost it.

1. Preheat oven to 325°F. Lightly butter and dust with flour a 12-cup Bundt or fluted tube pan. Tap out excess flour.

2. Line almonds in bottom of prepared pan evenly.

3. In a medium saucepan over low heat, warm coffee, margarine or butter, and chocolate chips, stirring constantly until chips have melted. Remove from heat; stir in sugar and almond extract until combined. Set aside for a few minutes until mixture cools down.

4. Into a large bowl, pour warm coffee mixture and, with a hand-held electric mixer set on low speed, beat in flour, baking soda, vanilla, and vinegar until completely combined.

5. Pour over almonds and bake for 45 to 55 minutes or until toothpick inserted in center comes out clean.

6. Cool in pan on wire rack for 10 minutes, then turn out onto serving plate and dust with confectioners' sugar.

Fudge Coconut Cake

CAKE

3 cups unbleached all-purpose
  flour

¾ cup unsweetened cocoa
  powder

1 teaspoon baking soda

2 teaspoons baking powder

1¾ cups granulated sugar

½ cup vegetable oil

1 (3⅝-ounce) package instant
  chocolate pudding filling

1 cup hot coffee or water

1 cup buttermilk

2 teaspoons vanilla extract

FILLING

1 (8-ounce) package cream
  cheese, softened

⅓ cup granulated sugar

1½ teaspoons vanilla extract

1 tablespoon vegetable oil

½ cup nuts, chopped

½ cup flaked coconut

1 (6-ounce) package semisweet
  chocolate chips

GLAZE

1 cup confectioners' sugar

3 tablespoons unsweetened
  cocoa powder

2 tablespoons butter, softened

2 teaspoons vanilla extract

1 to 3 tablespoons hot water

I love the combination of chocolate and coconut. It makes this a truly special cake.

1. *TO PREPARE CAKE:* Preheat oven to 350°F. Lightly butter and dust with flour a 12-cup Bundt or fluted tube pan. Tap out excess flour.

2. In a large bowl, with a handheld electric mixer set on medium speed, combine flour, cocoa, baking soda, baking powder, sugar, oil, and chocolate pudding. Beat in hot coffee, buttermilk, and vanilla until smooth. Set aside.

3. *TO PREPARE FILLING:* In a small bowl, with a handheld electric mixer set on medium speed, beat cream cheese, sugar, vanilla extract, and oil. By hand, fold in nuts, coconut, and chocolate chips. Set aside.

4. *TO ASSEMBLE CAKE:* Pour half of batter into prepared pan. Carefully spoon cream cheese filling over batter (filling should not touch sides or center of pan). Spoon remaining batter over cream cheese mixture.

5. Bake on center rack of oven for 55 to 65 minutes or until toothpick inserted in center comes out clean. Cool on wire rack 15 minutes; invert onto serving plate.

6. *TO PREPARE GLAZE:* In a small bowl, with a handheld electric mixer set on low speed, beat in confectioners' sugar, cocoa, butter, vanilla, and hot water (add more water if needed for desired consistency). Drizzle over cake and serve.

Phyllis's Date Nut Cake

1½ cups water

1 cup raisins

2 cups sugar

2 teaspoons baking powder

1¼ teaspoons baking soda

1 teaspoon vanilla extract

1 teaspoon ground cloves

1 teaspoon ground cinnamon

3 cups unbleached all-purpose flour

1 cup vegetable oil

1 cup chopped pitted dates

1 cup chopped walnuts

⅓ cup cold water

This cake is absolutely loaded with nuts and goodies. It's a great cake to keep in the freezer and take out for a holiday or other special occasion.

1. Preheat oven to 325°F. Lightly butter a 9¼ x 5 x 2½-inch loaf pan.

2. In a 2-quart saucepan with burner set on high, add 1½ cups water, raisins, sugar, baking powder, baking soda, vanilla, cloves, and cinnamon. Stirring constantly, allow to come to a boil and remove from stove. Set aside to cool slightly.

3. Meanwhile, in a large bowl, sift flour and combine with vegetable oil, chopped dates, chopped walnuts, and ⅓ cup cold water. With a wooden spoon, stir, then slowly add raisin mixture until completely mixed.

4. Pour into prepared pan and bake for 1 hour or until top is browned. Cool completely on wire rack.

Spicy Yeast Loaf Cake

YEAST MIXTURE

1 (¼-ounce) package active dry
  yeast
½ teaspoon sugar (to dissolve
  yeast)
⅔ cup warm water
¼ cup unbleached all-purpose
  flour

BATTER

1¼ cups raisins
2 tablespoons unbleached all-
  purpose flour (to coat raisins)
  plus 4 cups, sifted
1 cup plus 2 tablespoons butter or
  margarine
2¼ cups sugar
3¼ teaspoons baking powder
½ teaspoon ground nutmeg
½ teaspoon ground cinnamon
Pinch of salt
1¼ cups skim milk
½ cup nuts, chopped (optional)

This looks like a pound cake with raisins and has a delicate crumb. I found it in an old cookbook, removed the eggs, and made it better than the original, tasting like an expensive bakery cake.

1. Lightly butter and dust with flour two 8¼ x 4½ x 2½-inch metal loaf pans. Tap out excess flour.

2. *TO PREPARE YEAST MIXTURE:* In a measuring cup, combine yeast, sugar, and warm water until dissolved; stir in ¼ cup flour to make a thin mixture, and set aside in a warm place for 30 minutes until mixture starts to get frothy.

3. Preheat oven to 350°F (325°F if you are using an ovenproof glass pan).

4. *TO PREPARE BATTER:* Toss raisins and 2 tablespoons flour into a plastic bag and shake to coat raisins evenly with flour. Set aside.

5. In a large bowl, with a handheld electric mixer set on medium speed, beat butter or margarine and sugar until fluffy.

6. In a separate bowl, mix remaining 4 cups sifted flour with baking powder, nutmeg, cinnamon, and salt. Set aside. To butter-sugar mixture, gradually add flour mixture ½ cup at a time alternately with the milk, beginning and ending with dry ingredients, and mixing after each addition. With a wooden spoon, stir in yeast mixture and fold in raisins and nuts (if used). If batter is too thick, add a little more milk.

7. Pour batter evenly into prepared pans. Bake for 50 minutes or until golden brown.

8. Cool for 10 minutes in pans on wire racks. Remove and cool on wire racks.

Mouthwatering Orange Cake

makes 20 servings

CAKE

½ cup butter or margarine, room
   temperature

1 cup sugar

½ cup no-fat sour cream or
   yogurt

2 teaspoons vanilla extract

2¼ cups unbleached all-purpose
   flour

3 teaspoons baking powder

1 teaspoon baking soda

1 tablespoon grated orange peel

¼ cup orange juice concentrate,
   thawed

¼ cup vegetable oil

ORANGE GLAZE

½ cup orange juice

1 teaspoon orange extract

½ cup sugar

2 tablespoons orange liqueur
   (optional)

The recipe name says it all. Serve this with yogurt or ice cream. Sensational!

1. *TO PREPARE CAKE:* Preheat oven to 350°F. Lightly butter and dust with flour a 12-cup Bundt pan. Tap out excess flour.

2. In a large bowl, with a handheld electric mixer set on medium speed, cream butter or margarine and sugar together for 3 minutes until fluffy. With mixer at same speed, beat sour cream or yogurt, vanilla, flour, baking powder, baking soda, orange peel, orange juice concentrate, and oil. Mix for another 3 minutes until smooth.

3. Pour batter into prepared pan and bake for 30 to 35 minutes. Cool in pan on wire rack for 10 minutes.

4. *TO PREPARE GLAZE:* In a small saucepan over low heat, stir orange juice, orange extract, and sugar until a light syrup forms, approximately 5 minutes (stir in liqueur if used). Turn cake onto a serving dish and, with a toothpick, prick holes in the top of the cake 1 inch apart. Drizzle the orange glaze over the cake so that it sinks into the holes and serve.

Peach Blueberry Upside Down Cake

¾ cup firmly packed brown sugar

½ cup butter or margarine, room
  temperature

1 (29-ounce) can sliced peaches,
  well drained

½ cup drained fresh or frozen
  blueberries

2½ cups unbleached all-purpose
  flour

1¼ cups granulated sugar

1¼ tablespoons baking powder

½ teaspoon baking soda

1 teaspoon ground cinnamon

1¼ cups club soda

¼ cup applesauce

2 teaspoons vanilla extract

TOPPING

½ cup heavy whipping cream

2 tablespoons confectioners'
  sugar

1 teaspoon vanilla extract

This cake is very pretty and delicious. People will think you bought it at an expensive bakery. It's easier to make than you'd imagine. It is a big hit every time!

1. *TO PREPARE CAKE:* Preheat oven to 350°F. Lightly butter sides only of a 9-inch round springform pan.

2. In a small saucepan, on low heat, cook brown sugar and butter or margarine until melted; or in a microwave-safe bowl, melt butter and sugar in microwave on high setting for 1 minute.

3. Spread brown sugar mixture evenly on bottom of pan. Arrange peaches and blueberries over brown sugar mixture in a circular fashion. Put foil under pan to catch drippings.

4. In a large mixing bowl, combine flour, sugar, baking powder, baking soda, and cinnamon; with a wooden spoon, mix well; stir in club soda, applesauce, and vanilla until smooth.

5. Spread batter over peach slices evenly and bake for 40 to 45 minutes or until a wooden toothpick inserted in center comes out clean.

6. Cool in pan on wire rack 45 minutes, turn carefully upside down onto plate. Cool completely.

7. *TO PREPARE TOPPING:* In a small bowl, beat whipping cream, confectioners' sugar, and vanilla until stiff peaks appear.

8. Spoon out in clumps on top of peaches and blueberries, spacing far enough apart so that fruit will show.

Peach Liqueur Cobbler Brunch Cake

1 cup granulated sugar

¼ cup cornstarch

2 cups unbleached all-purpose
flour

3 teaspoons baking powder

2 teaspoons baking soda

1 (29-ounce) can peach slices in
heavy syrup (reserve syrup)

⅔ cup reserved peach syrup

2 tablespoons peach liqueur

1 tablespoon lemon juice

1 cup light sour cream

TOPPING

¼ cup butter or margarine

¼ cup firmly packed brown sugar

½ cup unbleached all-purpose
flour

2 teaspoons baking powder

1 teaspoon ground cinnamon

1 teaspoon peach liqueur

GLAZE

¼ cup confectioners' sugar

2 teaspoons peach liqueur

This cake is great to serve to a crowd. It's a cross between a cake and a cobbler.

1. Preheat oven to 350°F. Lightly butter a 9 x 13-inch non-stick pan.

2. In a large bowl, combine sugar, cornstarch, flour, baking powder, and baking soda. With a wooden spoon, stir until just combined. Add peach syrup, peach liqueur, lemon juice, and sour cream. Stir until smooth.

3. Pour into prepared pan and arrange peach slices in rows evenly on top. Press down slightly. Set aside.

4. *TO PREPARE TOPPING:* In a small bowl, combine butter or margarine, brown sugar, flour, baking powder, cinnamon, and peach liqueur. With a pastry blender or fork, blend until it resembles a crumbly mixture.

5. Sprinkle evenly over top of batter in pan and bake for 30 minutes or until toothpick inserted in center comes out clean.

6. Cool in pan on wire rack for 30 minutes. Invert onto a square serving plate.

7. *TO PREPARE GLAZE:* In a small mixing bowl, blend confectioners' sugar and liqueur. After cake is completely cooled, drizzle over top with a spoon.

Fat-Free and Delicious Pear-Carrot Cake

makes 16 servings

Vegetable oil cooking spray

1¼ cups shredded carrots

4 large pears, cored and diced
(approximately 3 cups)

2 teaspoons baking soda

3½ teaspoons baking powder

2 teaspoons ground cinnamon

½ teaspoon ground nutmeg
(optional)

3 cups unbleached all-purpose
flour

1½ cups granulated sugar

1 cup water

3 teaspoons vanilla extract

½ cup raisins (optional)

½ cup chopped nuts (optional)

Confectioners' sugar (to dust on
top)

Most of my recipes have variations for making fat-free versions. However, this absolutely delicious cake has no fat to begin with and because there are no eggs it has no cholesterol either.

1. Preheat oven to 350°F. Spray a 12-cup Bundt or fluted pan with vegetable oil cooking spray until completely coated.

2. Into a large bowl, add shredded carrots and diced pears. Then add baking soda, baking powder, cinnamon, nutmeg (if used), flour, sugar, water, and vanilla. Fold in raisins and/or nuts if used. With a wooden spoon, stir until completely mixed. Pour batter into prepared pan and bake for 35 to 40 minutes until toothpick inserted in center comes out clean.

3. Cool in pan on wire rack for 10 minutes, then invert onto a serving platter. Dust cake with confectioners' sugar and serve.

Aunt Jane's Pistachio Cake

Vegetable oil cooking spray

3 cups unbleached all-purpose
flour

1½ cups sugar

¼ cup vegetable oil

2 teaspoons vinegar

3 teaspoons baking powder

1½ teaspoons baking soda

2 cups lemon soda

½ cup light sour cream

2 teaspoons vanilla extract

1 (3.4-ounce) package instant
pistachio pudding filling

2 drops green food coloring
(optional)

1 cup pistachio nuts, shelled and
chopped

This delicious cake comes out dark and the variation is green. Both are well worth the effort.

1. Preheat oven to 350°F. With vegetable oil cooking spray coat a 12-cup Bundt pan.

2. With a handheld electric mixer set on medium speed, combine flour, sugar, oil, vinegar baking powder, baking soda, lemon soda, sour cream, vanilla, food coloring (if used), and pudding mix for 3 minutes. Fold in nuts.

3. Pour out into prepared pan. Bake for 35 to 45 minutes or until toothpick inserted in center comes out clean.

4. Cool in pan on a wire rack for 15 minutes before turning over onto a plate.

VARIATION

1 standard-size yellow cake mix

¾ cup unbleached all-purpose
flour

¼ cup sugar

1 (3.4-ounce) package pistachio
pudding

1 teaspoon baking soda

2 cups lemon or club soda

¾ cup light sour cream or plain
yogurt

1 cup chopped walnuts

Variation
Short-cut version.

1. Preheat oven to 350°F. Lightly butter a 12-cup Bundt pan.

2. In a large bowl, with a handheld electric mixer set on medium speed, beat cake mix, flour, sugar, pudding mix, baking soda, lemon soda, and sour cream for 3 minutes or until smooth. With a wooden spoon, fold in nuts.

3. Pour batter into prepared pan and bake for 50 to 55 minutes until sides come away from pan. Cool in pan on wire rack for about 15 minutes, then invert onto plate.

Butter Pound Cake

3¼ cups unbleached all-purpose
   flour

2 cups sugar

2 teaspoons baking powder

1 teaspoon baking soda

1 tablespoon vinegar

1½ cups buttermilk

1 cup butter or margarine, room
   temperature

2 teaspoons vanilla extract

BUTTER SAUCE

¾ cup sugar

¼ cup butter or margarine, room
   temperature

3 tablespoons water

2 teaspoons vanilla extract

This one is delicious. My friend Donna has three sons who all love this cake and they are very particular about what they eat. After you've had this pound cake you will never go back to those with eggs in them.

1. Preheat oven to 325°F. Lightly butter and dust with flour 12-cup Bundt or fluted tube pan. Tap out excess flour.

2. In a large bowl, with a handheld electric mixer set on low speed, beat flour, sugar, baking powder, baking soda, vinegar, buttermilk, butter or margarine, and vanilla until completely moistened; then beat 3 minutes at medium speed until smooth.

3. Pour batter into prepared pan and bake for 55 to 65 minutes or until toothpick inserted in center comes out clean. Cool in pan on wire rack for 10 minutes, then turn out onto serving plate.

4. *TO PREPARE BUTTER SAUCE:* In a small saucepan, over low heat, stir sugar, butter or margarine, water, and vanilla just until everything is combined and melted. Pour over cake.

Poppy Seed Pound Cake

2 tablespoons vegetable oil

1 cup butter or margarine, room temperature

2 tablespoons poppy seeds

1 tablespoon light corn syrup

1 cup sugar

2 cups unbleached all-purpose flour

1 teaspoon vanilla extract

1 teaspoon grated lemon peel

1 tablespoon lemon juice

2 teaspoons baking powder

3 teaspoons baking soda

½ cup no-fat sour cream

This is for the poppy seed lover. It is a wonderful-tasting traditional cake. Like the old-fashioned types of cakes, it is slightly heavy but moist.

1. Preheat oven to 350°F. Lightly butter and dust with flour a 12-cup Bundt pan. Tap out excess flour.

2. In a large bowl, with a handheld electric mixer set on low speed, combine vegetable oil and butter or margarine. Beat until smooth (approximately 1 minute). Stop mixer and add poppy seeds, corn syrup, sugar, flour, vanilla, lemon peel, lemon juice, baking powder, baking soda, and sour cream. Beat for 3 minutes on medium speed until lumps are gone and batter is smooth.

3. Pour into prepared pan and bake for 30 to 40 minutes until golden. Cool in pan on wire rack for 10 minutes, then turn out onto serving plate and cool completely before serving.

NOTE: You can substitute ½ cup of margarine for ½ cup sour cream for a lighter cake.

Lemony Whole-Wheat Poppy Seed Cake

¼ cup vegetable oil

½ cup honey

⅔ cup plain low-fat yogurt

3 tablespoons grated lemon rind

2 tablespoons lemon juice

1 teaspoon vanilla extract

1½ cups whole-wheat flour

½ cup quick rolled oats

1 teaspoon baking powder

1 teaspoon baking soda

½ cup poppy seeds

Old-fashioned and heart-warming, with a crunchy, delicious crust.

1. Preheat oven to 350°F. Lightly butter a 10-cup Bundt pan.

2. In a large bowl, combine oil, honey, yogurt, lemon rind, lemon juice, vanilla, whole-wheat flour, oats, baking powder, baking soda, and poppy seeds. With a wooden spoon, stir ingredients until completely mixed. Pour batter into prepared pan and bake for 30 minutes until golden brown.

3. Cool in pan on wire rack for 10 minutes, then invert onto serving platter.

Golden Pineapple Pound Cake

1 cup sugar

½ cup butter or margarine, room
temperature

½ cup low-fat sour cream

2¾ cups unbleached all-purpose
flour

3 teaspoons baking powder

1½ teaspoons baking soda

1 (3.4-ounce) package instant
vanilla pudding mix

1½ tablespoons cornstarch

1 teaspoon vanilla extract

1 (10-ounce) can crushed
pineapple or chunks (reserve
liquid)

¾ cup reserved pineapple juice,
adding water if necessary to
equal ¾ cup

¼ cup vegetable oil

TOPPING

1 (8-ounce) container whipped
topping

1½ pints heavy cream

1 (16-ounce) can crushed
pineapple (reserve liquid)

½ cup reserved pineapple juice

1 (3.4-ounce) package vanilla
instant pudding

⅓ cup dark rum

1 (3¾-ounce) package flaked
coconut

This one is rich and delicious. It cracks at the top when done, just like a pound cake should.

1. *TO PREPARE CAKE:* Preheat oven to 350°F. Lightly butter a 12-cup Bundt pan.

2. In a large bowl, combine sugar, butter or margarine, and sour cream. With a handheld electric mixer set on medium speed, beat until creamy. Then add flour, baking powder, baking soda, vanilla pudding, cornstarch, vanilla, crushed pineapple, pineapple juice, and oil. Beat for 3 minutes until smooth.

3. Pour into prepared pan and bake for 40 to 45 minutes or until golden. Cool on wire rack for 20 minutes before removing from pan.

4. *TO PREPARE TOPPING:* In a large bowl, with a handheld electric mixer set on medium speed, beat whipped topping and heavy cream together until thick (do not overbeat). On low speed, beat in pineapple juice, pudding, and rum and continue beating until well blended. Carefully fold in crushed pineapple and coconut and spread on cake when completely cooled.

Vermont Maple Walnut Cake

makes 10 to 12 servings

1 cup pure maple syrup

1¼ cups unbleached all-purpose flour

¼ cup sugar

1 tablespoon vegetable oil

1 cup milk

2½ teaspoons baking powder

1 teaspoon baking soda

2 tablespoons butter or margarine, room temperature

½ cup walnuts, finely ground (to sprinkle on top)

My friend Cindy adores this recipe. It has an old-fashioned taste and is just the type of cake a person with an allergy to eggs usually pines for.

1. Preheat oven to 400°F. Lightly butter a 9 x 9-inch pan.

2. In a 1-quart saucepan, heat maple syrup on high heat to bring to a boil. Pour into prepared cake pan.

3. In a large bowl, combine flour, sugar, oil, milk, baking powder, baking soda, and butter or margarine. With a wooden spoon, stir until completely mixed (add more milk if too thick).

4. Pour batter into pan over syrup. Bake for 20 to 30 minutes or until golden.

5. Cool in pan on wire rack for 10 minutes, turn out onto serving plate, and sprinkle with nuts.

Luscious Yellow Cake

2 cups sugar

1 cup vegetable oil

3½ cups unbleached all-purpose
  flour

2 teaspoons baking powder

1 teaspoon baking soda

2 teaspoons vinegar

½ cup milk

½ cup club soda

2½ teaspoons vanilla extract

The top of this cake comes out very crunchy and golden. It's great plain or topped with ice cream and fruit.

1. Preheat oven to 350°F. Lightly butter and dust with flour a 12-cup Bundt pan. Tap out excess flour.

2. In a large bowl, with a handheld electric mixer set on low speed, beat in sugar and oil. Add flour, baking powder, baking soda, vinegar, milk, club soda, and vanilla, beating approximately 3 minutes until smooth, scraping the sides with a spatula.

3. Pour batter into prepared pan and bake for 50 to 55 minutes or until golden.

4. Cool in pan on rack for 10 minutes, then turn out onto cake plate.

Yogurt Bismark Cake

¼ cup butter or margarine, room temperature

1 cup sugar

1 cup no-fat yogurt

1⅔ cups sifted unbleached all-purpose flour

2 teaspoons baking powder

1½ teaspoons baking soda

2½ teaspoons vanilla extract

This is not quite a pound cake and has a wholesome pure vanilla flavor. The title originated because, you guessed it, it sank! But everyone insisted it was a keeper! I almost sank myself, but instead, I lightened the ingredients and now it is an unsinkable must-try.

1. Preheat oven to 350°F. Lightly butter and dust with flour a 9 x 5 x 3-inch loaf pan. Tap out excess flour.

2. In a large bowl, with a handheld electric mixer set on medium speed, cream butter, sugar, and yogurt together until light and fluffy. Slowly add flour, baking powder, baking soda, and vanilla and beat on high for 3 minutes until batter is creamy-looking.

3. Pour batter into the prepared pan and bake for 30 to 40 minutes or until toothpick inserted in center comes out clean.

4. Cool the cake in its pan on wire rack for 20 minutes, then turn out onto plate.

VARIATION

1 box standard yellow cake mix, pudding included

1½ cups ginger ale

⅓ cup vegetable oil

1 teaspoon baking powder

5 to 6 tablespoons unbleached flour

Variation

This is a quick version of the previous cake using a boxed cake, if you really must cheat.

1. Preheat oven to 350°F. Lightly butter a 12-cup Bundt cake pan.

2. In a large bowl, combine cake mix, ginger ale, vegetable oil, baking powder, and flour. With a handheld electric mixer set on medium speed, beat for 3 minutes until creamy.

3. Pour into prepared cake pan and bake for 30 to 40 minutes. Cool for 20 minutes in pan on wire rack. Remove from pan and cool completely before serving.

Silver White Cake

1½ cups granulated sugar

2¾ cups unbleached all-purpose flour

1½ tablespoons baking powder

2 teaspoons baking soda

2 tablespoons white vinegar

½ cup vegetable oil

2 teaspoons vanilla extract

1 teaspoon almond extract

2 cups cold water

FOR TROPICAL ISLAND FROSTING

1 (8-ounce) package cream cheese

½ cup milk

1 (3.8-ounce) package instant vanilla pudding

TOPPING

1 cup whipped cream

1 tablespoon confectioners' sugar

1 (10-ounce) can pineapple rings, drained

1 cup flaked coconut

This is better than boxed cake and, of course, the egg-free part goes without saying.

1. *TO PREPARE CAKE:* Preheat oven to 375°F. Lightly butter a 9 x 13-inch pan.

2. In a large bowl, add sugar and flour, baking powder, baking soda, then make 3 wells. In one put vinegar, in another add oil, and in last well add extracts. Pour water over whole thing and, with a wooden spoon, mix.

3. Pour batter into prepared pan and bake for 30 to 40 minutes or until toothpick inserted in center comes out clean.

4. Cool in pan on wire rack for 10 minutes, then turn out onto a serving plate and cool completely.

5. *TO PREPARE FROSTING:* In a medium bowl, combine cream cheese, milk, and pudding. With a handheld electric mixer set on medium speed, beat for 3 minutes until thick. Spread over top and sides of cooled cake.

6. *TO PREPARE TOPPING:* In a separate bowl, combine whipped cream and confectioners' sugar. With a handheld electric mixer set on medium speed, beat until peaks form. Spread over cake on top of cream cheese mixture. Sprinkle with coconut and arrange drained pineapple rings on top.

Chocolate Cream Cheese Layered Cupcakes

CREAM CHEESE MIXTURE

2 (8-ounce) packages cream
  cheese, room temperature

⅓ cup sugar

1 teaspoon cornstarch

1 (6-ounce) package semisweet
  chocolate chips

CUPCAKE BATTER

1½ cups unbleached all-purpose
  flour

1 cup sugar

¼ cup unsweetened cocoa
  powder

1½ teaspoons baking soda

1 cup water

¼ cup vegetable oil

1 tablespoon vinegar

1 teaspoon vanilla extract

TOPPING

½ cup chopped almonds

1 tablespoon sugar

These are a crowd-pleaser among adults and kids alike.

1. Preheat oven to 350°F. Line with cupcake paper, twelve 3 x 1¼-inch (3½- to 4-ounce) muffin cups.

2. *TO PREPARE CREAM CHEESE MIXTURE:* In a small bowl, with a handheld electric mixer set on medium speed, beat cream cheese, sugar, and cornstarch until smooth. With a wooden spoon, fold in chocolate chips; set aside.

3. *TO PREPARE CUPCAKE BATTER:* In a large bowl, combine flour, sugar, cocoa, and baking soda and mix well; add water, oil, vinegar, and vanilla; with a handheld electric mixer set on medium speed, beat for 2 minutes.

4. Fill paper-lined muffin cups half full with cupcake batter.

5. Top each with a tablespoon of cream cheese mixture.

6. *TO PREPARE TOPPING:* In a separate small bowl, combine almonds and sugar and stir until combined; sprinkle evenly over cream cheese mixture.

7. Bake 20 to 25 minutes or until cream cheese is light golden brown.

8. Remove from pans and cool completely on wire racks.

I Cannot Believe It Has No Eggs Cheesecake

CRUST

1½ cups finely crushed chocolate
  cookie crumbs or graham
  cracker crumbs

½ cup margarine, melted

2 tablespoons sugar

FILLING

1 (8-ounce) package regular
  cream cheese, room
  temperature

2 (8-ounce) packages low-fat
  cream cheese, room
  temperature

½ cup sweetened condensed milk

½ cup sugar

¼ teaspoon baking soda

2 teaspoons baking powder

¼ cup cornstarch

1 tablespoon lemon juice

½ teaspoon grated lemon rind
  (optional)

1 tablespoon vanilla extract

1 pint (16 ounces) light sour
  cream

My crowning glory. This cheesecake is absolutely well worth the effort. It is truly delicious, and no one can tell the difference from one that has no eggs. It's very creamy, delicious, awesome, and great-tasting. Definitely judge this one by the title. Definitely make two and freeze one. It freezes well.

1. *TO PREPARE CRUST:* In a small bowl, combine chocolate cookie crumbs, melted margarine, and sugar; blend well. Press into bottom of an ungreased 9-inch springform pan. Put foil around bottom of pan so it does not drip. Set aside.

2. Preheat oven to 300°F.

3. *TO PREPARE FILLING:* In a large bowl, with a handheld electric mixer set on medium speed, beat cream cheese, condensed milk, sugar, baking soda, baking powder, cornstarch, lemon juice, lemon rind (if used), and vanilla. Beat until smooth, approximately 3 minutes. Add sour cream; blend well. Pour into prepared pan.

4. Bake for 1 hour, on center rack. Knife inserted in outer side of cake should come out clean when cake is done. Middle will still be creamy.

5. Turn off oven and open door; let cake sit in oven for another 2 to 3 hours to cool slowly.

6. Remove from oven after it has cooled, loosen sides of pan with a knife, and remove sides of pan. Place on a plate and allow to cool completely at room temperature before placing it in refrigerator (so it does not create condensation) covered with plastic wrap. Refrigerate for a couple of hours before serving.

Variations

You may use 4 (8-ounce) bars of light or regular cream cheese and 1 cup (8 ounces) sour cream instead of 16 ounces of sour cream for a slightly thicker cake. Or, for a softer cake use ¾ cup sweetened condensed milk and ¼ cup sugar and ⅓ cup cornstarch. It is great in either of these variations.

Creamy, Lemony, Heavenly New York Cheesecake

CRUST

1½ cups graham cracker crumbs

¼ cup sugar

½ cup margarine, melted

FILLING

1 pint (16 ounces) low-fat sour cream

3 tablespoons lemon juice

1 teaspoon vanilla extract

1 (3.4-ounce) package lemon pudding or pie filling

2 (8-ounce) packages low-fat cream cheese, room temperature

1¼ cups sugar

1 pound low-fat ricotta or small-curd cottage cheese, strained

⅓ cup cornstarch

1 teaspoon baking powder

½ teaspoon grated lemon rind

This cheesecake has a yellow coloring because there is lemon rind and lemon pudding in it. It has a more lemony taste than the previous recipe. Both are out of this world. Serve plain or topped with fresh fruit.

1. *TO PREPARE CRUST:* In a 10-inch springform pan, stir in graham cracker crumbs, sugar, and melted margarine until crumbs are moist, then pat down, making an even layer of moist cracker crumbs. Put foil around bottom of pan so it does not drip. Set aside.

2. *TO PREPARE FILLING:* Preheat oven to 325°F.

3. In a small bowl, combine sour cream, lemon juice, vanilla, and lemon pudding mix. With a spoon, stir until combined. Set aside.

4. In a large bowl, with a handheld electric mixer set on high speed, blend cream cheese, sugar, and ricotta or cottage cheese until smooth for approximately 3 minutes.

5. Change to low speed and slowly add sour cream mixture, cornstarch, baking powder, and lemon rind. Mix well until creamy, scraping sides of bowl with spatula and making sure you mix evenly.

6. Pour into prepared pan and bake for 1 hour and 20 minutes, or until sides are firm.

7. Turn off oven, open door, and allow to cool in oven for 2 hours. Remove from oven, and continue to cool completely in pan at room temperature (approximately 1 hour) before refrigerating (this prevents condensation forming on the top of cake). Loosen cake from sides of pan with a knife before removing the sides. Place cake with bottom ring of pan still attached on plate. Cover with plastic wrap and refrigerate approximately 2 hours before serving.

Chocolate Angel Cream Pies

½ cup margarine or butter, room
  temperature

1¼ cups granulated sugar

1½ teaspoons vanilla extract

2½ cups unbleached all-purpose
  flour

¾ cup cocoa powder

1¼ teaspoons baking soda

1 teaspoon baking powder

¾ cup milk

¼ cup tonic water

1 tablespoon vegetable oil

FILLING

2¾ cups confectioners' sugar plus
  2½ tablespoons flour

2 tablespoons vanilla extract

½ cup vegetable shortening

¼ cup whipping cream

These resemble the famous old-fashioned little cakes also referred to as "whoopie pies" or chocolate cake sandwiches with cream in the center.

1. *TO PREPARE CAKES:* Preheat oven to 425°F. Butter two non-stick 10 x 15-inch jelly roll pans. Set aside.

2. With a handheld electric mixer set on low speed, cream margarine or butter and sugar until light. Add vanilla, flour, cocoa, baking soda, baking powder, milk, tonic water, and vegetable oil and continue to mix with a wooden spoon. Batter should be very thick (if it is not, add a small amount of flour).

3. Drop by tablespoonfuls onto pans, spacing 1½ inches apart. Cover pans with foil and bake 5 to 7 minutes until round and puffy.

4. Cool in pans on wire rack for 3 minutes before removing with a spatula. Cool completely on wire rack before filling.

5. *TO PREPARE FILLING:* In a large bowl, with a handheld electric mixer set on medium speed, beat confectioners' sugar and flour mixture, vanilla, vegetable shortening, and whipping cream together until creamy (add more whipping cream if necessary for consistency).

6. Spread a thick layer of filling on bottom cake layer, put top layer on, sandwich together, and eat.

Cookies, Brownies, and Bars

Almond Bonbon Cookies

4-ounce bar sweet cooking
  chocolate

2 tablespoons milk

¼ cup sugar

¾ cup margarine or butter,
  softened

2 teaspoons vanilla extract

2 cups unbleached all-purpose
  flour

1 (3½-ounce) tube almond paste

COATING (OPTIONAL)

sugar

These are rich and delicious and they freeze well.

1. Preheat oven to 350°F.

2. In a small microwave-safe bowl, combine chocolate and milk and place in microwave on high for 1 minute, stirring until smooth. Set aside.

3. In a large bowl, with a handheld electric mixer set on medium speed, beat in sugar and margarine or butter until light and fluffy. Blend in chocolate mixture and vanilla. Slowly add flour, mixing well.

4. Using a teaspoonful of dough, shape into round balls. Place 2 inches apart on ungreased cookie sheets. In palm of your hand, take ¼ teaspoonful of almond paste, and press or form dough around filling with your hands to cover the almond paste, forming a ball with the paste in the center.

5. Place in oven and bake for 8 to 10 minutes. Cool in pans on wire racks for 5 minutes.

6. Roll in sugar (if used) while warm.

Almond Cookies

1¾ cups unbleached all-purpose flour

½ cup sugar

¼ cup chopped toasted almonds

¾ cup margarine or butter, room temperature

½ cup vegetable shortening

½ cup canned almond paste

1 teaspoon double-acting baking powder

1 teaspoon vanilla extract

These are soft cookies with a really great taste.

1. In a large bowl, combine flour, sugar, almonds, margarine or butter, shortening, almond paste, baking powder, and vanilla. With a wooden spoon, stir until completely mixed.

2. Refrigerate for 45 minutes.

3. Meanwhile, preheat oven to 375°F.

4. Remove dough from refrigerator and drop by rounded teaspoonfuls onto ungreased cookie sheet, spacing 2 inches apart. Bake 10 minutes or until golden.

5. Cool in pan on wire rack for 3 minutes. Remove cookies onto wire racks and allow to cool completely.

Almond-Filled Cookies

¾ cup butter or margarine, room
temperature

1¾ cups unbleached all-purpose
flour

1 teaspoon baking powder

1 teaspoon baking soda

1 cup firmly packed light brown
sugar

⅓ cup quick rolled oats

1 teaspoon vanilla extract

5 ounces canned almond paste

Homemade cookies don't get any better than these! Pure heaven—crisp and delicious.

1. Preheat oven to 375°F. Lightly butter two cookie sheets.

2. In a large bowl, combine butter or margarine, flour, baking powder, baking soda, sugar, oats, and vanilla; with a handheld electric mixer set on low speed, beat until completely combined, approximately 3 minutes.

3. Take a teaspoon of dough and, using your hands, flatten into a circle ¼ inch thick and 2 inches in diameter. Place ¼ teaspoonful of almond paste in the center of the circle, fold in half, and seal edges with a fork. Repeat this process until dough is finished.

4. Place flattened dough on prepared cookie sheet 2 inches apart and bake for 7 to 10 minutes or until lightly browned.

5. Cool completely on wire rack in pan.

Almond Whole-Wheat Coconut Cookies

makes approximately
4 dozen cookies

½ cup butter or margarine, room
  temperature

¾ cup pure maple syrup or honey

1½ teaspoons vanilla extract

¼ teaspoon almond extract

1¼ cups whole-wheat flour

¾ cup unbleached all-purpose
  flour

1¼ teaspoons baking powder

¾ cup sweetened flaked coconut

½ pound almond paste, crumbled

Almond, maple syrup or honey, whole-wheat flour, and coconut make a yummy (and healthy) combination.

1. In a large bowl, with a handheld electric mixer set on medium speed, beat butter or margarine, maple syrup, and extracts. Set aside.

2. Sift dry ingredients slowly into wet mixture. Then, using a wooden spoon, blend in coconut and stir in crumbled almond paste.

3. Cover dough with plastic wrap and refrigerate for 20 minutes.

4. Meanwhile, preheat oven to 350°F. Lightly butter two baking sheets.

5. Remove dough from refrigerator. With your hands, roll dough into balls 1 inch in diameter and place 2 inches apart on cookie sheets. Bake for 12 to 15 minutes until lightly browned. Cool in pans on wire racks 5 minutes. Then remove cookies with spatula.

Butterscotch No-Fail Cookies

makes 4 to 6 dozen cookies

- 2½ cups unbleached all-purpose flour
- 1½ teaspoons baking soda
- 1 cup butter or margarine, room temperature
- ¾ cup firmly packed light brown sugar
- ¼ cup granulated sugar
- ½ cup water
- 1 (3.4-ounce) package butterscotch instant pudding/pie filling
- 1½ teaspoons vanilla extract
- 2 tablespoons vegetable oil
- 1 (11-ounce) package butterscotch bits
- 1 cup chopped walnuts (optional)

My friends and neighbors really rave about this one. This is a definite "better double the batch."

1. Preheat oven to 375°F.

2. In a large bowl, with a handheld electric mixer set on low speed, beat flour, baking soda, butter or margarine, sugars, water, pudding mix, vanilla, and oil until dough sticks together, approximately 3 minutes.

3. Fold in butterscotch bits and nuts (if used); batter will be very stiff. Drop by teaspoonfuls 2 inches apart onto ungreased cookie sheets. Bake 8 minutes. Cool completely on wire rack before removing from pan.

Chocolate Brownie Drop Cookies

1⅓ cups vegetable shortening

2 tablespoons vanilla extract

⅔ cup granulated sugar

1 cup firmly packed brown sugar

2⅓ cups unbleached all-purpose
  flour

2 teaspoons baking powder

1 teaspoon baking soda

⅔ cup plus 1 teaspoon cocoa
  powder

3 tablespoons milk

1 tablespoon vegetable oil

1½ cups walnuts or pecans,
  chopped

½ cup semisweet chocolate pieces

½ cup flaked coconut (optional)

These are truly rich cookies. When people eat them they can't stop, so make plenty.

1. Preheat oven to 350°F.

2. In a large bowl, with a wooden spoon, stir vegetable shortening, vanilla, sugars, flour, baking powder, baking soda, cocoa, milk, oil and mix thoroughly until smooth. Then fold in nuts, chocolate, and coconut (if used).

3. Drop dough by rounded teaspoonfuls onto ungreased baking sheet 2½ inches apart. Bake for 7 to 8 minutes. Cool 2 minutes on baking sheet. Remove and place on wire racks to cool completely.

Sophisticated Chocolate Hazelnut Cookies

4 ounces unsweetened or semisweet chocolate

1¼ cups butter or margarine, softened

1 cup confectioners' sugar

¼ cup granulated sugar

1½ teaspoons vanilla extract

2 cups unbleached all-purpose flour

1 cup toasted hazelnuts, chopped

This is a fine European-style soft cookie. Hazelnuts have a subtle, rich flavor. These are a must-try. You can toast hazelnuts in oven for about 5 minutes at 350°F.

1. In top of a double boiler over hot water, melt chocolate, stirring occasionally until smooth. Remove top part of double boiler and cool chocolate until warm. To microwave, in a microwave-safe bowl, melt chocolate on high setting for 1 minute or until melted, remove and stir until smooth. Set aside until warm.

2. In a large bowl, using a wooden spoon, cream together butter or margarine and sugars until smooth; stir in cooled chocolate and vanilla. Slowly add flour and mix thoroughly. Fold in nuts.

3. Place a piece of plastic wrap approximately 2 feet long on a work surface.

4. Scrape dough into center of plastic wrap and roll with your hands to form a log approximately 2 inches in diameter and 16 inches long.

5. Wrap plastic around log and refrigerate for 2 hours until dough becomes hard enough to slice.

6. Remove dough from refrigerator. Take off plastic wrap and place on a hard work surface.

7. Preheat oven to 350°F.

8. With a sharp knife, cut dough into ½-inch-thick diagonal slices. Place them on 2 ungreased baking sheets spacing them 2 inches apart. Bake for 10 to 12 minutes.

9. Remove from oven and cool on wire racks in pans.

Loaded Chocolate Chip Cookies

½ cup butter or margarine, room temperature

⅓ cup granulated sugar

½ cup firmly packed light brown sugar

1½ cups unbleached all-purpose flour

1 teaspoon baking soda

2 teaspoons vanilla extract

3 tablespoons vegetable oil

1 to 2 tablespoons water if needed

½ cup chopped nuts (optional)

1 (6-ounce) package semisweet chocolate pieces

½ cup shredded coconut (optional) (delicious)

This particular chocolate chip cookie goes over with a bang. I triple the recipe and roll the dough in a long 1-inch-round log, so when I'm in a hurry I just take one out of the freezer and slice it into ½-inch-thick slices and bake. They also freeze well.

1. Preheat oven to 350°F.

2. In a large bowl, with a handheld electric mixer set on medium speed, cream butter or margarine and sugars until fluffy, approximately 2 minutes. Slowly sift in flour and baking soda. Add vanilla and oil and mix until completely combined (for a flatter cookie, or if batter is still too dry, add 1 to 2 tablespoons of water).

3. With a wooden spoon, fold in nuts (if used), chocolate, and coconut (if used).

4. Drop by rounded teaspoonfuls on ungreased cookie sheets spaced 2 inches apart and bake for 8 to 10 minutes. Cool on wire racks in pans for 3 minutes. Remove with a spatula and transfer onto wire racks and cool completely.

Choc Full of Chocolate Chips

1¼ cups butter or margarine,
  room temperature

1¾ cups sugar

¼ cup quick rolled oats

2 cups unbleached all-purpose
  flour

1 cup cocoa powder

1 teaspoon baking soda

2 tablespoons vegetable oil

1½ cups chocolate chips

1 cup nuts (your choice), chopped

This cookie is definitely for the chocolate lover.

1. Preheat oven to 350°F.

2. In a large bowl, with a handheld electric mixer set on medium speed, cream butter or margarine and sugar. Add oats, flour, cocoa, baking soda, oil, and fold in chocolate chips and nuts.

3. Drop by rounded teaspoonfuls on ungreased cookie sheets and bake for 8 to 10 minutes until slightly golden.

4. Cool 3 minutes on cookie sheets then remove to wire racks to cool completely.

chocolate Kiss cookies

1 (14-ounce) package milk
  chocolate kisses
1 cup butter or margarine, room
  temperature
¼ cup granulated sugar
¼ cup firmly packed light brown
  sugar
1½ teaspoons vanilla extract
2 cups unbleached all-purpose
  flour

This cookie tastes great and is very nice-looking as well.

1. Preheat oven to 375°F. Remove wrappers from milk chocolate kisses. Set aside.

2. In a large bowl, with a handheld electric mixer set on medium speed, beat butter or margarine, sugars, and vanilla. Slowly add flour, blend until smooth.

3. Mold 1 tablespoon of dough around each chocolate piece to cover completely. Shape into balls.

4. Place on ungreased cookie sheet and bake 10 to 12 minutes or until set.

5. Cool slightly in pan on wire rack; remove from cookie sheet to wire rack. Cool completely.

Chocolate Kiss in Apricot Cookies

1 (14-ounce) package milk chocolate candy kisses

1 cup butter or margarine, room temperature

1 (4.5-ounce) package chocolate pudding and pie filling mix

1 tablespoon vegetable oil

1 teaspoon baking powder

2 cups unbleached all-purpose flour

3 tablespoons sugar (for coating)

¼ cup apricot preserves

TOPPING (OPTIONAL)

½ cup semisweet chocolate chips

3 tablespoons margarine or butter, melted

This combination of chocolate and apricot is absolutely delicious.

1. Preheat oven to 325°F. Remove wrappers from candy. Set aside.

2. In a large bowl, with a handheld electric mixer set on medium speed, beat butter or margarine, pudding mix, and oil until combined. Slowly beat in baking powder and flour at low speed until dough forms; shape into 1-inch balls. Roll in sugar to coat. Place 2 inches apart on ungreased cookie sheets.

3. Make a thumbprint in each ball and fill with ¼ teaspoon of preserves, then place candy kisses in the center.

4. Place in oven on center rack and bake for 10 to 15 minutes until slightly golden. With spatula, remove cookies from pans onto wire racks to cool.

5. *TO PREPARE OPTIONAL TOPPING:* In a microwave-safe bowl, put chocolate chips and margarine or butter. Place in microwave on high setting for 1 minute or until chips and margarine are completely melted; stir occasionally.

6. Drizzle ½ teaspoon topping over each cookie and allow to cool completely.

Variation

In place of apricot preserves you may substitute raspberry preserves.

Chocolate Puffs

3 (1-ounce) squares unsweetened
   chocolate

1¼ cups butter or margarine,
   room temperature

½ cup skim milk

2 teaspoons vanilla extract

1 cup firmly packed brown sugar

2 cups unbleached all-purpose
   flour

1 teaspoon baking powder

1 teaspoon baking soda

½ cup crispy rice cereal

Granulated sugar (to sprinkle on
   top)

This cookie is crispy and delicious (and, of course, chocolatey).

1. In a microwave-safe bowl, melt chocolate and butter or margarine in microwave for 1 minute on high setting. Stir until blended. Remove from heat and stir in milk, vanilla, and sugar. Set aside.

2. In a large bowl, combine flour, baking powder, baking soda, and crispy rice cereal. With spoon, stir to mix. Pour in chocolate mixture and, with a wooden spoon, stir until it forms a stiff dough. Cover and place in refrigerator for 1 hour.

3. Preheat oven to 350°F. Remove dough from refrigerator and uncover.

4. On ungreased cookie sheets, drop dough by rounded teaspoonfuls 2 inches apart. Sprinkle with sugar just to coat lightly.

5. Bake for 8 to 10 minutes.

6. Cool on cookie sheets on wire racks for 1 minute. Then carefully remove cookies to cool completely on wire racks.

Black and White Chocolate Cookies

1¼ cups vegetable shortening

¾ cup granulated sugar

⅔ cup firmly packed brown sugar

2 tablespoons vanilla extract

3 tablespoons vegetable oil

2¼ cups unbleached all-purpose flour

⅔ cup cocoa powder

2 teaspoons baking soda

1 teaspoon baking powder

4 tablespoons milk

2¼ cups whole walnuts, almonds, or pecans

½ cup semisweet chocolate pieces

¼ cup white chocolate baking pieces

¼ cup flaked coconut (optional)

These are absolutely awesome—an old-fashioned cookie that people can't seem to stop eating. Perfect for a crowd.

1. Preheat oven to 350°F.

2. In a large bowl, with a wooden spoon, combine shortening, sugars, and vanilla; stir until creamy. Add oil, flour, cocoa, baking soda, baking powder, and milk, stirring until completely smooth. Fold in walnuts, almonds, or pecans, chocolate pieces, and coconut (if used).

3. Onto two ungreased baking sheets, drop tablespoonfuls of dough, using 2 tablespoonfuls to form 1 cookie; space 3 inches apart. Bake 8 to 10 minutes. Cool 2 minutes in pans on wire racks, then remove from pans onto wire racks to cool completely.

Healthy Chocolate Cinnamon Nut Cookies

¾ cup butter or margarine, room
   temperature

½ cup honey

½ cup firmly packed light brown
   sugar

3 teaspoons vegetable oil

2 teaspoons vanilla extract

1¾ cups whole-wheat flour

⅓ cup cocoa powder

3 teaspoons baking powder

COATING

2½ cups walnuts, finely chopped

1 teaspoon ground cinnamon

½ cup confectioners' sugar

These get rave reviews from the kids—especially fresh out of the oven.

1. In a large bowl, with a handheld electric mixer set on medium speed, beat butter or margarine, honey, brown sugar, oil, and vanilla for 3 minutes until creamy. With a wooden spoon, stir in slowly flour, cocoa, and baking powder, blending until dough is smooth. Cover with plastic wrap and place in refrigerator for 1 hour.

2. Preheat oven to 350°F. Lightly butter 2 baking sheets.

3. Remove dough from refrigerator, unwrap, and with your hands roll into balls 1-inch in diameter.

4. *TO PREPARE COATING:* In a small bowl, combine nuts and cinnamon. In a separate small bowl, place confectioners' sugar. Roll balls in nut mixture first, then in confectioners' sugar, coating them heavily. Place on prepared cookie sheets 3 inches apart.

5. Bake for 13 to 15 minutes until they flatten. On wire racks, cool cookies on sheets slightly, then remove quickly with a spatula so they do not stick to pan. Cool completely on wire racks.

Fig Fantastic Cookies

makes approximately
3 dozen cookies

1 cup or 1 (8-ounce) package
  dried figs

½ cup sugar

½ cup margarine, room
  temperature

1 teaspoon grated orange peel

1 cup unbleached all-purpose
  flour

1½ teaspoons baking powder

½ cup walnuts, chopped
  (optional)

1 tablespoon orange juice

These are soft, and pure ecstasy! I recommend making them with the nuts.

1. Preheat oven to 375°F. Lightly butter baking sheet.

2. In your blender or chopper, finely chop figs. (Consistency will be like thick pulp.)

3. In a large bowl, combine figs, sugar, margarine, and orange peel; with a fork, cream together until smooth. Add flour, baking powder, walnuts (if used), and orange juice; continue mixing with fork until well blended.

4. Drop dough by rounded teaspoonfuls 1 inch apart on prepared cookie sheet.

5. Bake for 8 to 10 minutes until slightly browned. Cool on wire rack in pan for 1 minute, then remove with a spatula to wire rack to cool completely.

Betty's Gingersnap Cookies

2¾ cups unbleached all-purpose
 flour

1 tablespoon ground cinnamon

1 teaspoon ground cloves

1 teaspoon ground ginger

1 teaspoon baking soda

¾ cup firmly packed light brown
 sugar

⅔ cup butter or margarine, room
 temperature

3 tablespoons water

3 tablespoons light molasses

1 teaspoon lemon extract

These are great-tasting cookies.

1. In a large bowl, mix flour, spices, baking soda, and sugar. With a wooden spoon, stir in butter or margarine until combined; add water, molasses, and lemon extract. Mix thoroughly.

2. Cover bowl with plastic wrap, chill overnight.

3. Preheat oven to 350°F. Light butter 2 cookie sheets.

4. Using a rolling pin, roll out dough to ⅛-inch thickness and cut with your favorite cookie cutters. Repeat until all dough is used up.

5. Place dough on prepared cookie sheets ½ inch apart. Bake for approximately 8 minutes. Cool on wire racks in pans 2 minutes, then remove with spatula to wire racks to cool completely.

Peggy's Gingerbread Cookies

makes 2 dozen cookies
or 1 small gingerbread
house or mold

½ cup vegetable shortening

½ cup granulated sugar

½ cup dark molasses

2 tablespoons cold water

3 cups unbleached all-purpose
  flour

1¼ teaspoons ground ginger

1 teaspoon ground cinnamon

Vegetable oil cooking spray
  (optional)

FROSTING

¾ cup confectioners' sugar

3 ounces cream cheese, softened

3 tablespoons corn syrup

½ teaspoon vanilla extract

Raisins (for decorating)

This recipe can be used for cookies, as a mold, or for gingerbread houses. For cookies, simply roll dough out to ¼-inch thickness and cut with your favorite cookie cutters. It's delicious!

1. In a large bowl, with a handheld electric mixer set on medium speed, cream shortening, sugar, molasses, and water. Slowly add flour, ginger, and cinnamon. Mix well until stiff dough forms. Chill for 1 hour.

2. Preheat oven to 350°F. Lightly butter or spray a gingerbread house mold with vegetable spray. Press dough into mold and bake for 25 minutes. Cool for 5 minutes and carefully remove from mold piece by piece to cooling rack to completely cool flat side down. It is better to bake gingerbread 1 day in advance, then assemble following day. Assemble with frosting below to hold mold together.

3. *FOR NON-MOLD DIRECTIONS:* Simply roll out gingerbread to ¼-inch thickness, cut each piece with your favorite cookie cutters, and bake for 20 to 25 minutes. Allow to cool in pan for 5 minutes before removing to wire racks. Decorate as you wish.

4. *TO PREPARE FROSTING:* In a medium bowl, with a handheld electric mixer set on medium speed, combine confectioners' sugar, cream cheese, corn syrup, and vanilla and mix until desired consistency.

5. Frost cookies as creatively as you wish, using a butter knife to spread frosting. Use raisins as eyes and nose, by pressing them in while cookie is still soft. This frosting also holds mold or gingerbread house together. Spread it between pieces you are trying to hold together. Use it like glue.

Michael's Favorite Soft Molasses Cookies

2½ tablespoons margarine, room
temperature

1 tablespoon vegetable oil

½ cup firmly packed light brown
sugar

⅔ cup light molasses

2 tablespoons light corn syrup

3¼ cups unbleached all-purpose
flour

Pinch of salt

1 teaspoon ground cinnamon

1 teaspoon baking soda

¼ cup water

½ cup raisins, chopped

1 teaspoon granulated sugar (to
sprinkle on top)

This cookie puffs up and crackles on the top and remains soft. My son would eat a whole batch if we let him.

1. In a medium bowl, with a handheld electric mixer set on medium speed, beat margarine, oil, and brown sugar until combined; turn on low speed and add molasses and corn syrup.

2. Slowly add flour, salt, and cinnamon. In a measuring cup, mix baking soda with water until it is dissolved, pour into batter, and beat another 2 minutes on medium speed until a soft somewhat sticky dough is formed. Fold in raisins.

3. Chill dough for 1 hour until firm (not sticky). Flour your hands and turn dough out onto a lightly floured surface; roll into a long log 2-inches in diameter. Cut into ¾-inch-thick slices.

4. Preheat oven to 375°F. Lightly butter 2 cookie sheets.

5. Place slices on prepared cookie sheets 2 inches apart. Bake for 8 to 12 minutes until firm. Sprinkle with sugar. Cool on cookie sheets for 1 minute, then remove to wire racks and cool completely.

Italian Cookies

3 cups unbleached all-purpose flour

1 heaping teaspoon double-acting baking powder

1¼ cups granulated sugar

1 cup butter or margarine, room temperature

1 tablespoon vanilla or lemon extract

3 tablespoons orange juice

6 tablespoons anise (or Sambuca) liqueur

GLAZE

½ box confectioners' sugar

1 tablespoon butter or margarine, melted

1 tablespoon vanilla extract or ½ tablespoon Sambuca

Milk

This is an old Italian cookie recipe that has been around for generations. It is a cakey cookie, the taste is light, and you get the flavor of the liqueur or extract.

1. In a large bowl, combine flour, baking powder, sugar, butter or margarine, vanilla extract, orange juice, and liqueur.

2. Using your hands, knead batter in bowl until all ingredients are well blended and dough sticks together. (If it does not, add drops of water until it does. If dough is too sticky, add a little flour until it does not stick to your hands.)

3. Preheat oven to 350°F. With your hands, roll dough into 1-inch balls. Place on ungreased cookie sheets 1 inch apart. Bake 12 to 16 minutes or until lightly browned on bottom. Remove to wire racks to cool in pans 3 minutes and remove from pans with spatula to cool completely on wire racks.

4. *TO PREPARE GLAZE:* In a large bowl, with a handheld electric mixer set on medium speed, beat in sugar with melted butter or margarine. Add vanilla or Sambuca; then add milk to desired consistency.

Caitlin's Favorite Jelly Cookies

⅔ cup sugar

¾ cup margarine or butter, room temperature

1 tablespoon vegetable oil

2 teaspoons vanilla extract

¼ cup water

1 teaspoon baking powder

2 cups unbleached all-purpose flour

½ cup red raspberry jam or favorite preserves

Delicious cookies that also freeze well. Easy to make, and everyone raves about these cookies, including my daughter, Caitlin, who inspired this book in the first place.

1. Preheat oven to 350°F.

2. In a large bowl, with a handheld electric mixer set on medium speed, beat sugar, margarine or butter, oil, and vanilla; slowly add water until smooth. With a wooden spoon, stir in baking powder and flour; mix well until dough sticks together and forms into a ball. Divide dough into 4 equal parts.

3. On lightly floured surface, shape each wedge into a 12 x ¾-inch log; place on ungreased cookie sheets. Using handle of wooden spoon or your finger, make a depression about ½ wide and ¼ inch deep, lengthwise down the center of each log. Fill each with 2 tablespoons of jam. Bake for 10 to 15 minutes or until light golden brown. Cool slightly, then cut them in diagonals ½ inch thick. Cool completely on wire racks.

Dream Jam Pastry Cookies

2¼ cups unbleached all-purpose
   flour

½ cup sugar

1 teaspoon baking powder

¼ cup butter or margarine, room
   temperature

¼ cup vegetable shortening

¾ cup whipping cream

1 cup jam (¼ cup strawberry, ¼
   cup blueberry, ¼ cup peach, ¼
   cup apricot, or any combination
   of your choice to make 1 cup)

These are scrumptious.

1. In a large bowl, combine flour, sugar, and baking powder; with a pastry blender, cut in butter or margarine and vegetable shortening until crumbly.

2. In a separate bowl, beat cream until stiff and stir into flour mixture, blending well to make a stiff dough. Divide dough into 4 balls. Wrap each dough ball in plastic wrap and chill several hours or overnight.

3. With a floured rolling pin, roll out dough 1 ball at a time to an 8-inch square on a floured pastry board; cut into sixteen 2-inch squares.

4. Spoon a rounded ¼ teaspoon of jam in middle of each square. Fold all 4 corners to center. Dip tip of your finger in water, moisten dough where you are sealing it, and press lightly to seal. Or, only fold 2 corners to center, sealing with a tiny bit of water to moisten; press lightly and leave 2 ends open.

5. Preheat oven to 350°F. Lightly butter 2 cookie sheets.

6. Place 1 inch apart on prepared cookie sheets. Bake 15 to 18 minutes or until firm and lightly golden. Remove cookie sheets; cool completely on wire racks.

Kevin's Favorite Walnut Cookies

¼ cup semisweet chocolate chips, melted

½ cup unbleached all-purpose flour

¼ granulated sugar

½ cup butter or margarine, room temperature

1 teaspoon baking powder

½ teaspoon baking soda

2 teaspoons vanilla extract

1½ cups chopped walnuts

½ cup shredded coconut

½ cup chocolate chips

Confectioners' sugar (to sprinkle on top)

These are chock full of nuts, crisp and delicate.

1. Preheat oven to 350°F. Lightly butter cookie sheets.

2. In a small saucepan, on low heat, stir chocolate until completely melted. Set aside. Or put chocolate in a microwave-safe bowl and place in microwave on high setting for 1 minute. Remove and stir until smooth. Set aside.

3. In a large bowl, with a handheld electric mixer set on medium speed, beat melted chocolate, flour, sugar, butter or margarine, baking powder, baking soda, and vanilla. Fold in nuts, coconut, and chocolate chips.

4. Drop by rounded teaspoonfuls ½ inch apart onto cookie sheets; bake for 10 minutes, remove cookie sheet to a wire rack. When cooled, sprinkle with confectioners' sugar.

Phyllis's Hungarian Cookies

2 (8-ounce) packages cream
cheese

1 pound (4 sticks), butter or
margarine, room temperature

4 cups unbleached all-purpose
flour

½ teaspoon vanilla extract

½ teaspoon baking powder

FILLINGS

1 (8 ounce) can nuts (any kind)

1 (8-ounce) can apricot filling

1 (8-ounce) can cherry filling

1 (8-ounce) can blueberry filling

These are an old–fashioned Hungarian cookie—a traditionally eggless recipe.

1. In a large bowl, with a handheld electric mixer set on medium
speed, beat cream cheese and butter or margarine until soft;
gradually add flour, vanilla, and baking powder until well mixed.
Make 4 balls out of dough; wrap each ball with plastic and refrigerate I hour.

2. Preheat oven to 375°F. On a floured board, roll each ball out
to ¼-inch thickness; cut in squares, and drop ½ teaspoon of each
filling (nuts, apricots, cherries, and blueberries) on each square.
Fold 2 corners of each square over, using water on your finger to
seal edges closed, leaving top and bottom opened.

3. Place on ungreased, non-stick pan and bake for approximately
IO to I2 minutes until golden.

Variation
(Aunt Jane's Recipe)

Use ½ pound (2 sticks) of butter and ½ pound (I cup) of veg-
etable shortening instead of just butter or margarine.
I teaspoon baking powder instead of ½ teaspoon.
Do not add vanilla.
Bake in a 450°F oven for 5 minutes or until slightly golden. You
have to watch them closely because they burn quickly.

Lemon Cookie Lights

2 cups unbleached all-purpose
  flour

2 cups mashed potato flakes

1 cup granulated sugar

1 cup firmly packed brown sugar

2 cups chopped nuts

1 teaspoon baking soda

¾ cup butter or margarine,
  melted

1 tablespoon vegetable oil

⅓ cup water

2 teaspoons grated lemon peel

1 tablespoon lemon juice

COATING

¼ cup granulated sugar

These are nice and crisp, and great-tasting too!

1. Preheat oven to 350°F.

2. In large bowl, with a large fork, combine flour, mashed potato flakes, sugars, nuts, baking soda, butter or margarine, oil, water, lemon peel, and lemon juice until well mixed.

3. Firmly press mixture into 1-inch balls; roll in ¼ cup sugar to coat. Place 2 inches apart on ungreased cookie sheets.

4. Bake for 9 minutes or until golden brown.

5. Immediately remove from pans.

Mouthwatering Coconut Cookies

makes 2 dozen cookies

1½ cups unbleached all-purpose
   flour

2¼ tablespoons cornstarch

½ cup confectioners' sugar

1 cup butter or margarine

¼ cup nuts (optional)

½ cup mini-chocolate morsels
   (optional)

COATING

1½ cups flaked coconut

A friend of mine brought these cookies over and I just had to take out the eggs and make it myself!

1. In a large bowl, with a handheld electric mixer set on low speed, slowly blend in flour, cornstarch, confectioners' sugar, and butter or margarine. Fold in nuts and morsels (if used). Refrigerate for 1 hour.

2. Meanwhile, preheat oven to 300°F.

3. Shape into 1-inch balls, roll in coconut; place 2 inches apart on ungreased baking sheet. Bake for 20 minutes or until lightly browned. Immediately remove from pan onto wire racks.

Honey Oatmeal Coconut Raisin Cookies

makes 6 dozen cookies

1½ cups vegetable shortening
   (room temperature)

1 teaspoon butter flavor extract

1 cup granulated sugar

½ cup firmly packed brown sugar

½ cup honey

¼ cup milk

1 teaspoon vanilla extract

2½ cups unbleached all-purpose
   flour

1 teaspoon baking soda

1 teaspoon baking powder

1 cup quick rolled oats

1 cup flaked coconut

2 cups raisins

½ cup walnuts or almonds
   (optional)

The combination of honey, brown sugar, coconut, and raisins adds a wonderful flavor to this cookie.

1. Preheat oven to 375°F.

2. In a large bowl, with a wooden spoon, cream shortening, butter extract, sugars, honey, milk, vanilla, flour, baking soda, baking powder, and quick oats. Fold in coconut, raisins, and nuts (if used).

3. Drop rounded teaspoonfuls of dough 2 inches apart on ungreased baking sheets. Bake for 10 minutes.

JoAnne's Oatmeal Cookies

makes approximately
2½ dozen cookies

¾ cup vegetable shortening

2 tablespoons vegetable oil

1 cup firmly packed brown sugar

½ cup granulated sugar

¼ cup water

1 tablespoon vanilla extract

3 cups quick rolled oats

1 cup unbleached all-purpose
   flour

1½ teaspoons baking soda

1 cup raisins

2 (1-ounce) squares baking
   chocolate, melted

1 cup chopped nuts

JoAnne always made the best cookies I have ever tasted. This is a delicious eggless variation.

1. Preheat oven to 325°F. Lightly butter 2 cookie sheets.

2. In a large bowl, with a handheld electric mixer set on medium speed, mix together shortening, oil, sugars, water, and vanilla until creamy; slowly add oats, flour, baking soda, raisins, and melted chocolate, and mix well.

3. Drop by rounded teaspoonfuls on prepared cookie sheets spacing 1 inch apart.

4. Bake 15 minutes. Remove from baking sheets onto wire racks for 3 minutes then remove with spatula to cool completely.

Orange Drop Cookies

2¾ cups unbleached all-purpose flour

½ cup butter or margarine, room temperature

½ cup applesauce

1 cup sugar

1 tablespoon grated orange peel

¼ teaspoon orange extract

¼ teaspoon vanilla extract

1 teaspoon baking soda

Red and green sprinkles (optional)

These are cookies to complement any table. Serve with tea or coffee.

1. Preheat oven to 375°F. Lightly butter 2 cookie sheets.

2. In a large bowl, with a handheld electric mixer set on medium speed, beat flour, butter or margarine, applesauce, sugar, orange peel, extracts, and baking soda. Drop by rounded teaspoonfuls 2 inches apart on prepared cookie sheets.

3. Decorate with red and green sprinkles if desired. Bake 10 to 15 minutes or until lightly browned. Cool on wire racks in pan for 3 minutes and remove cookies with a spatula to wire racks to cool completely.

Orange Coconut Brittle Cookies

makes 2½ dozen cookies

1 cup unbleached all-purpose
  flour

1 cup quick rolled oats

1 cup firmly packed brown sugar

1 teaspoon baking soda

1 teaspoon baking powder

½ cup vegetable shortening

1 tablespoon grated orange peel

⅓ cup orange juice concentrate,
  thawed

½ cup chopped nuts (optional)

¼ cup flaked coconut

I love the flavor of orange and coconut together. This cookie is a big hit.

1. Preheat oven to 350°F. Lightly butter 2 cookie sheets.

2. In a large bowl, combine flour, rolled oats, sugar, baking soda, and baking powder; with a spoon, stir until combined. With a handheld electric mixer set on medium speed, beat in shortening, orange peel and orange juice concentrate until completely mixed. Fold in chopped nuts (if used) and coconut until well blended.

3. Drop by rounded teaspoonfuls 2 inches apart onto prepared cookie sheets.

4. Bake for 10 minutes, remove from cookie sheets, and cool.

Pistachio Balls

2¼ cups unbleached all-purpose
flour

1¾ cups butter or margarine,
room temperature

1 teaspoon vegetable oil

¾ cup confectioners' sugar

1 teaspoon vanilla extract

⅔ cup lightly salted pistachio
nuts, shelled and finely chopped

COATING

½ cup confectioners' sugar

These cookies are a great addition to a variety of cookies on a plate or by themselves. They're great-tasting.

1. In a large bowl, combine flour, butter or margarine, oil, confectioners' sugar and vanilla until blended. With a wooden spoon, stir until completely smooth. Fold in nuts and blend completely. Cover with plastic wrap and refrigerate 2 hours.

2. Preheat oven to 375°F. Lightly butter 2 baking sheets.

3. Between your hands, shape dough into balls 1 inch in diameter. Place balls on prepared baking sheets, spacing 1 inch apart.

4. Bake 10 to 15 minutes or until tops are set and bottoms are lightly browned.

5. Meanwhile, put confectioners' sugar in a pie tin.

6. Remove baking sheets to wire rack and cool cookies for 2 minutes.

7. Carefully roll cookies in confectioners' sugar to coat. Handle delicately.

Delicious Poppy Seed Cookies

2 cups unbleached all-purpose
  flour

⅔ cup sugar

1½ teaspoons baking powder

⅓ cup poppy seeds

½ cup applesauce

½ cup butter or margarine, room
  temperature

2 teaspoons vanilla extract

3 tablespoons vegetable oil

2 tablespoons grated lemon rind
  (optional)

Poppy seeds are good for digestion. These make a good snack.

1. Preheat oven to 350°F. Lightly butter 2 baking sheets.

2. In a large bowl, combine flour, sugar, baking powder, poppy seeds, applesauce, butter or margarine, vanilla, oil, and lemon rind (if used). With a handheld electric mixer set on medium speed, blend ingredients together until smooth.

3. Make little balls about ½ inch round by rolling between your hands; place 2 inches apart on prepared cookie sheets. You can bake them like that or press them down with a glass to flatten them a little. Bake until golden brown, approximately 15 to 20 minutes.

4. Remove from sheets immediately and cool on wire racks.

Variation
You may use caraway instead of poppy seeds.
¼ cup flaked coconut may be added after the lemon rind.
¼ cup chopped nuts may be added after the lemon rind.

Caraway-Brandy Royalty Cookies

1 cup unbleached all-purpose
flour

1½ teaspoons baking powder

¼ cup margarine or butter, room
temperature

½ cup granulated sugar

1 tablespoon vegetable oil

1 teaspoon caraway seeds

2 tablespoons brandy or ½
teaspoon brandy extract

2 teaspoons grated lemon zest

2 teaspoons lemon extract
(optional)

2 tablespoons confectioners'
sugar (to dust)

This cookie is fit for kings and queens. It is crisp and unusual-tasting, with a nice lemon flavor.

1. In a small bowl, stir together flour, baking powder, margarine or butter, sugar, oil, caraway seeds, brandy or brandy extract, lemon zest and lemon extract (if used) until the mixture forms a firm dough. Pat into a ball, wrap with plastic, and place in refrigerator or 1 hour until firm (this makes it easier to roll out).

2. Preheat oven to 375°F. Take out 2 cookie sheets.

3. Remove dough from refrigerator and roll out on a very lightly floured surface to ¼-inch thickness. Cut with a 1-inch round cookie cutter. Reroll scraps until all dough is used. Place ½ inch apart on ungreased cookie sheets.

4. Bake in oven for 8 to 10 minutes, until bottoms are browned. Remove to rack to cool. Dust with confectioners' sugar when cooled.

Plain Butter Cookies

makes approximately
4 dozen cookies

1 cup butter or margarine, room
 temperature

1 cup confectioners' sugar, sifted

1½ teaspoons vanilla extract

2⅓ cups unbleached all-purpose
 flour

Pinch of salt (optional)

These are crisp and delicious—a classic.

1. In a large bowl, with a handheld electric mixer set on medium speed, beat butter or margarine and confectioners' sugar together until smooth. Add vanilla, flour, and salt (if used). Continue to beat on medium speed until combined.

2. With your hands, shape into 2 balls, then roll each out like a log shape, approximately 2 inches in diameter and 12 inches long. Wrap with plastic wrap, place in refrigerator, and chill overnight.

3. Preheat oven to 400°F.

4. Remove from refrigerator and unwrap dough. With a sharp knife, cut into slices about ⅛ inch thick and place 1 inch apart on 2 ungreased cookie sheets.

5. Bake for 8 to 10 minutes. Let sit in pan for 1 minute, then remove to wire rack to cool completely.

Raspberry Butter Cookies

1 cup (2 sticks) sweet butter

¾ cup confectioners' sugar

1½ cups unbleached all-purpose flour

1 teaspoon baking powder

2 tablespoons cornstarch

1 cup finely chopped almonds or walnuts

½ cup raspberry preserves

These cookies taste like expensive butter cookies and with a taste of raspberry jelly on top.

1. In a large bowl, with a handheld electric mixer set on medium speed, cream butter and sugar until light and fluffy.

2. Slowly sift in flour, baking powder, cornstarch, and nuts until soft dough is formed.

3. Roll in a log 1½ inches in diameter and 8 inches long. Wrap with wax paper or plastic wrap and refrigerate until firm, approximately 2 to 3 hours. Remove dough from refrigerator and unwrap.

4. Preheat oven to 325°F.

5. Using a sharp knife, cut cookies ¼ inch thick and place cut side down on ungreased cookie sheets, spacing them 1 inch apart.

6. Bake cookies for 10 to 15 minutes until light brown around the edges.

7. Remove and cool in pans until set (approximately 1 to 2 minutes).

8. While the cookies are still cooling, spread ¼ teaspoon of raspberry preserves on half of each cookie.

Raspberry Oat Cookies

1 cup firmly packed brown sugar

¾ cup granulated sugar

1 cup margarine or butter, room temperature

¾ cup water

1 teaspoon almond extract

3 cups unbleached all-purpose flour

3 tablespoons vegetable oil

2 cups quick rolled oats

1 teaspoon baking soda

1 teaspoon baking powder

½ teaspoon ground cinnamon

½ cup flaked coconut (optional)

⅔ cup raspberry preserves

These cookies are always a great success—they fly right off the plate.

1. Preheat oven to 400°F.

2. In a large bowl, with a handheld electric mixer set on medium speed, beat sugars and margarine or butter until fluffy. Beat in water, almond extract, flour, and oil; blend well. Stop mixer and stir with spatula. Change to low speed; add oats, baking soda, baking powder, cinnamon, and coconut (if used).

3. Drop dough by rounded teaspoonfuls 2 inches apart onto ungreased cookie sheets. With back of spoon, make depression in center of each cookie. Fill each depression with ½ teaspoon of preserves. Drop scant teaspoonful of dough over preserves on each cookie.

4. Bake for 5 to 7 minutes or until light golden brown.

5. Remove from cookie sheets immediately onto wire racks to cool completely.

Russian Balls

¼ cup granulated sugar

1¼ cups butter or margarine, room temperature

1 cup almonds or walnuts, finely ground

2 cups unbleached all-purpose flour

Pinch of salt

2 tablespoons vanilla extract

COATING

½ cup confectioners' or granulated sugar

¾ teaspoon ground cinnamon (optional)

These are chock full of nuts. They are dipped in confectioners' sugar and they will just crumble right in your mouth. They're a favorite of many and are traditionally eggless.

1. In a large bowl, with a handheld electric mixer set on medium speed, cream sugar and butter or margarine until fluffy. Add ground nuts. Slowly add flour, salt, and vanilla. Continue beating until stiff dough forms.

2. Wrap dough in plastic wrap; refrigerate 1 hour until firm.

3. Preheat oven to 325°F.

4. Shape dough into balls. Place on 2 ungreased cookie sheets 1 inch apart; bake 15 to 20 minutes until set. Cool 10 minutes.

5. *TO PREPARE COATING:* In a pie tin, combine sugar and cinnamon (if used).

6. Roll cookies to coat them in sugar and cinnamon (if used) and place them on a serving dish.

Jan's Favorite Sweet Sesame Logs

makes approximately
4½ dozen logs

1¼ cups butter or margarine,
   room temperature
2½ teaspoons vanilla extract
¾ cup sugar
2½ cups unbleached all-purpose
   flour
2 cups sesame seeds, toasted

These cookies are a traditional holiday favorite. They have a great flavor and go well with coffee or tea.

1. Preheat oven to 350°F.

2. In a large bowl, combine butter or margarine, vanilla, and sugar. Beat with a handheld electric mixer set on medium speed until light and fluffy; slowly add flour and mix completely until smooth dough forms.

3. Put plastic wrap over top of bowl and chill dough in refrigerator approximately 1 hour.

4. Place sesame seeds on a 10 x 13-inch pan and bake for 20 to 25 minutes, stirring a couple of times to make sure they don't burn. Cool completely while you are waiting for dough to chill.

5. Remove dough from refrigerator. Pinch dough off about a teaspoon at a time. Roll into logs about 1 inch long and ½ inch wide; then roll each log in sesame seeds. Place logs on ungreased cookie sheets 1 inch apart.

6. Bake for 12 to 15 minutes until lightly browned. Cool completely.

Chocolate Shortbread Cookies

2 cups unbleached all-purpose
flour

½ cup plus ½ tablespoon
unsweetened cocoa powder

1 cup plus 2 tablespoons
confectioners' sugar, sifted

1 cup cold unsalted butter, cut
into small pieces

1¼ teaspoons vanilla extract

These cookies taste great, and kids especially love to use their favorite cookie cutters to make a fresh batch.

1. Preheat oven to 300°F.

2. In a large bowl, combine flour, cocoa, confectioners' sugar, butter, and vanilla. With a handheld electric mixer set on medium speed, beat 3 minutes until dough sticks together (add a little water if it does not stick together).

3. Remove dough from bowl and knead on a lightly floured board until dough is smooth.

4. With a lightly floured rolling pin, roll dough to a thickness of ½ inch.

5. Cut dough with shaped cookie cutters of your choice. Reroll scraps of dough to make more cookies. Place 1 inch apart on un-greased baking sheets.

6. Bake 16 to 20 minutes or until brown around edges. Remove cookies from pans and cool completely on wire racks.

Scottish Shortbread Cookies with Chocolate Coating

2¼ cups unbleached all-purpose flour

1 cup butter or margarine, room temperature

½ cup confectioners' sugar

¼ teaspoon salt

1 cup chocolate chips or chocolate mint candies

This is a rich cookie, similar to biscotti in texture, decked with chocolate.

1. Preheat oven to 325°F.

2. In a large bowl, combine flour, butter or margarine, sugar, and salt. With your hands, knead until well mixed.

3. Press dough into an ungreased 7 x 11-inch or 8 x 8-inch pan; prick 3 rows of holes with a fork.

4. Bake for 40 to 50 minutes or until golden brown.

5. Allow shortbread to cool in pan approximately 5 minutes, then cut into rectangles or squares.

6. While shortbread is cooling, in a small pan on medium heat, melt chocolate, stirring constantly until completely melted. Or put chocolate in microwave-safe bowl and place in microwave on high setting for 1 minute. Stop and stir until chocolate is melted. Cool slightly, then pour melted chocolate over cut shortbread.

7. Cool completely in refrigerator until chocolate hardens.

Simple Sugar Cookies

makes approximately
3 dozen cookies

4 cups unbleached all-purpose
  flour

4¾ teaspoons baking powder

¼ teaspoon salt

1 cup margarine or butter, room
  temperature

1¾ cups granulated sugar

½ cup water

2 teaspoons vanilla extract

TOPPING OR COATING

½ cup granulated or colored
  sugar (optional)

Kids love these old-fashioned sugar cookies. I make them for school parties.

1. In a large bowl, with a handheld electric mixer set on medium speed, beat flour, baking powder, salt, margarine or butter, sugar, water, and vanilla. Add a small amount of water if necessary to smooth.

2. Chill overnight.

3. Preheat oven to 375°F. Lightly butter 2 cookie sheets.

4. Roll dough out to ⅛-inch thickness; cut out with your favorite cookie cutters. Reroll scraps of dough to make more cookies.

5. Dip each cookie into granulated or colored sugar (if used) before placing on prepared cookie sheets 1 inch apart.

6. Bake for 8 to 10 minutes or until slightly browned. Remove from pans and cool on wire racks.

Almond Lemon Raspberry or Blueberry Squares

makes 12 squares

BASE

2 cups unbleached all-purpose
  flour

1 cup sugar

1 (3.9-ounce) package lemon
  pudding mix

2 teaspoons baking powder

2 teaspoons baking soda

½ cup butter or margarine, room
  temperature

¼ cup water

¼ cup light corn syrup

3 teaspoons lemon extract

FILLING

2 (3-ounce) packages cream
  cheese

¼ cup sugar

1 tablespoon cornstarch

2 teaspoons vanilla extract

1 tablespoon vegetable oil

1 cup frozen raspberries or
  blueberries

TOPPING

1 cup crumb mixture (reserved
  from base)

1 cup graham cracker crumbs

3 tablespoons butter or margarine

¼ cup water

These are scrumptious—a delicious treat.

1. Preheat oven to 350°F. Lightly butter a 9 x 13-inch pan.

2. *TO PREPARE BASE:* In a large bowl, combine flour, sugar, pudding mix, baking powder, baking soda, butter or margarine, water, corn syrup, and lemon extract. With a pastry blender, mix all ingredients together until they form a thick dough. (Reserve 1 cup.)

3. *TO PREPARE FILLING:* In a medium bowl, combine cream cheese, sugar, cornstarch, vanilla, and vegetable oil. With a hand-held electric mixer set on medium speed, mix until smooth. Set aside.

4. Press crumb mixture base into bottom of prepared pan, spread filling over that, and sprinkle raspberries or blueberries over that.

5. *TO PREPARE TOPPING:* In a small bowl, combine reserved crumb mixture from base and mix in graham cracker crumbs, butter or margarine, and water. Spread over raspberries or blueberries and bake for 35 to 40 minutes until golden brown.

Apple Spice Bars

½ cup butter or margarine, room
   temperature

1¼ cups sugar

¼ cup tonic water

1 cup unbleached all-purpose
   flour

1 teaspoon baking soda

1 teaspoon baking powder

1¼ cups quick rolled oats

2 tablespoons cocoa powder

1 teaspoon ground cinnamon

½ teaspoon ground nutmeg

¼ teaspoon ground cloves

2 cups chopped peeled apples

½ cup chopped nuts

These are tasty and look great served by themselves or with a bunch of other bars on a platter. The cocoa gives them a different flavor.

1. Preheat oven to 375°F. Lightly butter a 9 x 13 x 2-inch baking pan.

2. In a large bowl, with a handheld electric mixer set on medium speed, cream butter or margarine and sugar. Add tonic water, flour, baking soda, baking powder, rolled oats, cocoa, cinnamon, nutmeg, and cloves; mix well. Fold in chopped apples and nuts.

3. Spread batter in prepared pan.

4. Bake for 20 minutes or until done. Cool on wire rack. Cut into squares when cooled.

Apricot Squares

FILLING

⅔ cup dried apricot halves

⅓ cup water

1 cup firmly packed light brown sugar

⅓ cup unbleached all-purpose flour

1 teaspoon cornstarch

½ teaspoon baking powder

½ cup nuts, chopped

BASE

½ butter or margarine, room temperature

¼ cup granulated sugar

½ cup chopped almonds or walnuts

1 cup unbleached all-purpose flour

1 teaspoon baking powder

1 teaspoon vanilla extract

Confectioners' sugar (to sprinkle on top)

My friend Margaret gave this a rave review, and she is an excellent baker.

1. Preheat oven to 350°F. Lightly butter an 8 x 8-inch baking pan.

2. *TO PREPARE FILLING:* In a covered saucepan, over low heat, cook apricots and water for 15 minutes (or until water evaporates). Remove from heat, set aside, and cool slightly.

3. In a medium bowl, with a handheld electric mixer set on medium speed, beat in apricots, brown sugar, flour, cornstarch, baking powder, and nuts. Set aside.

4. *TO PREPARE BASE:* In a large bowl, with a handheld electric mixer set on medium speed, beat butter or margarine, sugar, nuts, flour, baking powder, and vanilla, until mixed.

5. Pat into prepared pan and bake 25 minutes or until golden. Pour apricot mixture over baked layer and bake 20 minutes longer.

6. Cool in pan; cut into squares when cooled. Sprinkle with confectioners' sugar and serve.

Blueberry Bars

2 (3-ounce) packages light cream
cheese

¼ cup butter or margarine, room
temperature

1¼ cups unbleached all-purpose
flour

½ teaspoon baking soda

¾ cup quick rolled oats

⅓ cup firmly packed brown sugar

1 teaspoon grated lemon peel

TOPPING

1 cup fresh blueberries or
blueberry jam

½ teaspoon lemon juice

1 cup reserved crumbs

To me there is nothing like blueberries. These bars are absolutely awesome.

1. Preheat oven to 350°F. Lightly butter a 9 x 9 x 2-inch baking pan.

2. In a large bowl, with a pastry blender, cut in cream cheese and butter or margarine until smooth. Cut in flour, baking soda, quick oats, brown sugar, and lemon peel until this resembles a crumb mixture (reserve 1 cup).

3. Pat remaining crumb mixture in bottom of prepared pan. Bake for 20 minutes.

4. *TO PREPARE TOPPING:* Meanwhile, in a medium bowl, mix blueberries and lemon juice. Spread over baked crust, sprinkle reserved crumbs on top of blueberry mixture, and bake another 10 minutes or until brown. Cool for 15 minutes in pan and cut into 2½-inch squares.

Butterscotch Bars

These sweet bars will definitely impress company or your family.

BASE

1 cup butter or margarine, room
   temperature

¾ cup firmly packed light brown
   sugar

⅓ cup water

1½ teaspoons vanilla extract

¾ teaspoon almond extract

2 cups unbleached all-purpose
   flour

TOPPING

1¼ cups butterscotch morsels

1¼ cups chopped almonds

¼ cup flaked coconut

¼ cup chocolate chips (optional)

1. Preheat oven to 350°F.

2. *TO PREPARE BASE:* With a handheld electric mixer set on medium speed, beat butter or margarine, sugar, water, and extracts until fluffy; slowly beat in flour and mix well.

3. Press batter into ungreased 9 x 13 x 2-inch pan.

4. *TO PREPARE TOPPING:* Sprinkle butterscotch morsels evenly over top of base, then sprinkle on nuts, coconut, and chocolate chips (if used) evenly and press lightly into cookie mix.

5. Bake in oven for 20 minutes. Cool completely in pan on wire rack before cutting.

Baklava

makes approximately 28 pieces

SYRUP

¾ cup water

1½ cups sugar

½ cup honey

¼ cup margarine

2 teaspoons lemon juice

½ teaspoon grated lemon peel

½ teaspoon granted orange peel

½ teaspoon ground cinnamon

FILLING

3 cups finely chopped walnuts

½ cup sugar

1½ teaspoons ground cinnamon

¼ teaspoon ground cloves

¼ teaspoon ground nutmeg

1 (1-pound) box phyllo dough,
   room temperature

10 ounces melted sweet butter

This is a classic Greek dessert with a flaky crust and a nutty sweet flavor. Time-consuming to prepare, but well worth it.

1. *TO PREPARE SYRUP:* In a medium saucepan, combine water, sugar, honey, margarine, lemon juice, lemon peel, orange peel, and cinnamon; bring to a boil and remove from heat.

2. *TO PREPARE FILLING:* In a medium bowl, stir nuts, sugar, cinnamon, cloves, and nutmeg. Set aside.

3. Brush a 9 x 13-inch pan with melted butter.

4. Unroll phyllo dough and line pan with 1 phyllo sheet. Brush evenly with butter and repeat with 6 more sheets, brushing each with melted butter.

5. Spread one third of filling evenly over top layer of pastry sheets. Cover filling with another 2 pastry sheets, brushing each with butter.

6. Spread another third of filling over pastry sheets and add 2 more phyllo sheets on top, brushing each with butter. Add remaining filling over sheets and cover with 8 more phyllo sheets, brushing each with butter.

7. With a sharp knife, mark the rectangle with 5 lengthwise and 7 diagonal markings for 28 diamond-shaped pieces and then cut them.

8. Preheat oven to 350°F.

9. Bake on center rack for 50 to 60 minutes. If dough gets too brown before that time, cover with aluminum foil.

10. Remove from oven and cool for 5 minutes. Pour cooled syrup evenly over hot baklava and allow to absorb syrup for 6 hours uncovered. If you cover it, that will cause pastry to become soggy.

11. Serve when completely cooled.

NOTE: Refrigerate leftovers.

Caramel Squares

BASE

2 cups unbleached all-purpose
  flour

2 teaspoons baking powder

1 teaspoon baking soda

2⅓ cups quick rolled oats

1½ cups tightly packed brown
  sugar

1 cup margarine or butter, melted

½ cup skim milk

2 teaspoons vinegar

TOPPING

1 (14-ounce) package caramels

¼ cup skim milk

1 cup nuts (your choice), chopped

These go over big. They taste as if you bought them in an expensive bakery—old-fashioned and definitely sweet.

1. Lightly butter and dust with flour a 13 x 9 x 2-inch pan. Tap out excess flour.

2. Preheat oven to 350°F.

3. *TO PREPARE BASE:* In a large bowl, combine flour, baking powder, baking soda, oats, and brown sugar. Stir in melted margarine or butter, milk, and vinegar until crumbly. Press half of crumbly mixture into prepared pan (reserve other half) and bake for 10 to 12 minutes. Remove from oven and set aside.

4. *TO PREPARE TOPPING:* In a 2-quart saucepan, over low heat, melt caramels in milk, stirring until smooth; remove from heat. Or place caramels and milk in a microwave-safe bowl and cover with plastic wrap with a couple of holes punched in it. Microwave on high setting for 1 to 2 minutes until melted. Set aside.

5. Sprinkle nuts over baked crumbly mixture and with a spatula scrape caramel mixture over nuts. Sprinkle remaining crumbly mixture over caramel mixture; press down slightly.

6. Bake for another 15 to 20 minutes or until lightly browned.

7. Cool in pan for 45 minutes, loosening sides with a spatula immediately.

8. Cut into 2-inch squares and cool completely before removing from pans.

Variation

You can also sprinkle ½ cup flaked coconut and I cup of chocolate chips over top before final baking for a richer taste for the holidays.

Caramel Cookie Bars

makes 48 bars

BASE

2 cups unbleached all-purpose
    flour

¾ cup confectioners' sugar

2 teaspoons corn syrup

1 cup butter or margarine, room
    temperature

¼ cup whipping cream

2 teaspoons baking powder

1 teaspoon baking soda

1¼ teaspoons vanilla extract

FILLING AND TOPPING

30 caramel candies

½ cup whipping cream

⅓ cup margarine or butter, room
    temperature

¾ cup confectioners' sugar

2 tablespoons cornstarch

2 cups chopped pecans

GLAZE

½ cup semisweet chocolate chips

3 tablespoons whipping cream

1 tablespoon butter or margarine,
    room temperature

⅓ cup confectioners' sugar

1¼ teaspoons vanilla extract

These bars are over the top on the sweet meter. They are sinfully delicious.

1. *TO PREPARE BASE:* Preheat oven to 325°F.

2. In a large bowl, with a handheld electric mixer set on medium speed, beat flour, confectioners' sugar, corn syrup, butter or margarine, whipping cream, baking powder, baking soda, and vanilla until crumbly. Press crumbly mixture into ungreased 15 x 10 x 1-inch baking pan and bake for 15 minutes or until golden.

3. *TO PREPARE FILLING AND TOPPING:* In small saucepan, over low heat, melt caramels in whipping cream and margarine or butter. Or place caramels, whipping cream, and margarine or butter in a microwave-safe bowl and cover with plastic wrap with a couple of holes punched in it. Microwave on high setting for 1 minute or until melted. Remove from heat (or microwave); stir in confectioners' sugar, cornstarch, and pecans (add additional cream if necessary for spreading consistency). Spread filling/topping over base. Set aside.

4. *TO PREPARE GLAZE:* In a small saucepan, over low heat, melt chocolate chips with 3 tablespoons whipping cream and 1 tablespoon or butter or margarine, stirring until smooth. Or place these ingredients in a microwave-safe bowl, cover with plastic wrap with a couple of holes punched in it, and microwave on high for 1 minute to melt chips. Remove from heat (or microwave); stir in confectioners' sugar and vanilla. Drizzle glaze over filling. Place in refrigerator for 2 hours until set.

cherry Delights

½ cup (1 stick) butter or
  margarine, room temperature

1 cup firmly packed light brown
  sugar

1 teaspoon almond extract

1 cup unbleached all-purpose
  flour

1½ teaspoons baking powder

1 cup quick rolled oats

1 tablespoon corn syrup

¾ cup cherry preserves

½ cup finely chopped almonds
  (optional)

These bars are absolutely chewy scrumptious. They go quickly so I would double the recipe.

1. Preheat oven to 350°F. Lightly butter an 8 x 8-inch baking pan.

2. In a medium bowl, with a fork, cream butter or margarine and sugar; add almond extract, flour, baking powder, oats, and corn syrup. Stir until crumbly. (Reserve 1 cup crumbly mixture in a separate bowl.) Spread remaining oat mixture evenly into prepared pan and press down firmly.

3. Spoon out preserves in center of pan and spread only within ¼ inch from edges of pan.

4. Add chopped nuts (if used) to reserved crumbly mixture; stir until mixed. Sprinkle crumbs evenly over top and pat down lightly.

5. Bake for 35 to 40 minutes until lightly browned.

6. Cool in pan before cutting.

Variation
You can use apricot, blueberry, orange, or your favorite preserves instead of cherry.

Chocolate Cream Cheese Bars

BASE

1 cup firmly packed brown sugar

½ cup butter or margarine, room temperature

½ cup sour cream, room temperature

2 teaspoons baking powder

1 teaspoon baking soda

2 cups unbleached all-purpose flour

½ cup almonds, finely chopped

FILLING AND TOPPING

1 (8-ounce) package cream cheese, room temperature

¾ cup granulated sugar

1 teaspoon vanilla extract

¼ cup cocoa powder

3 teaspoons milk

1 teaspoon cornstarch

½ cup mini-chocolate chips

1 cup base mixture (reserved)

Like a chocolate cheesecake inside a cookie bar, these are delicious!

1. Preheat oven to 350°F. Lightly butter an 8 x 8 x 2-inch pan.

2. In a large bowl, with a handheld electric mixer set on medium speed, beat sugar, butter or margarine, and sour cream together until smooth. Add baking powder, baking soda, flour, and nuts; mix until moist (reserve 1 cup).

3. Pat batter mixture into bottom of pan evenly.

4. *TO PREPARE FILLING AND TOPPING:* In a medium bowl, with a handheld electric mixer set on medium speed, beat cream cheese, granulated sugar, vanilla, cocoa powder, milk, and cornstarch until smooth. Spread cream cheese mixture evenly over mixture in pan; sprinkle evenly with mini-chocolate chips and spread reserved base mixture over that.

5. Bake for 35 to 40 minutes or until center is firm and top is golden brown.

6. Cool completely in pan (approximately 30 minutes). Cut into bars when cooled.

7. Transfer to a serving plate (do not stack them). Cover with plastic wrap and refrigerate ½ hour before serving.

Date Nut Bars

½ cup sugar

1 cup chopped dates

½ cup vegetable oil

¼ cup chopped walnuts

¾ cup unbleached all-purpose
flour

1½ teaspoons baking powder

This is a healthy lunch box snack.

1. Preheat oven to 350°F. Lightly butter an 8 x 8 x 2-inch pan.

2. In a large bowl, mix sugar, dates, oil, and nuts. Add flour and baking powder and mix well until smooth. Spread in prepared pan and bake for 20 minutes.

3. Remove, cool completely, then cut into bars.

Fun-Filled Cookie Bars

makes 24 bars

1¼ cups butter or margarine,
   room temperature
1 cup graham cracker crumbs
1 cup chocolate cookie crumbs
1 (14-ounce) can sweetened
   condensed milk
1 (6-ounce) package semisweet
   chocolate morsels
½ cup toffee crunch bar
   (crumbled or in package already
   crumbled)
½ cup shredded coconut
1 cup chopped walnuts

A wonderful holiday or special-occasion bar, this rich dessert is a favorite.

1. Preheat oven to 350°F.

2. In a 10 x 13 x 2-inch baking pan, melt butter or margarine in oven. Sprinkle graham cracker crumbs evenly over butter. Then sprinkle chocolate cookie crumbs over graham cracker crumbs; pat down again and make sure they are evenly spread in pan. Pour sweetened condensed milk evenly over chocolate crumbs.

3. Layer evenly each of remaining ingredients: semisweet chocolate morsels, toffee crunch bar crumbs, coconut, and nuts. Press down gently.

4. Bake for 25 to 30 minutes or until lightly browned. Cool completely in pan.

5. When cooled, cut into bars and serve.

Graham Cracker Bars

2¾ cups graham cracker crumbs

1 (14-ounce) can sweetened condensed milk

1½ tablespoons honey

3 tablespoons orange juice

¾ cup semisweet chocolate chips

Confectioners' sugar (to dust)

Graham crackers and chocolate make these terrific.

1. Preheat oven to 325°F. Butter a 9 x 13 x 2-inch pan.

2. In a medium bowl, combine crumbs, condensed milk, honey, and orange juice; with a wooden spoon, mix well. Stir in chocolate chips.

3. Spread batter evenly in prepared pan. Bake for 20 to 30 minutes or until lightly browned and sides come away from pan.

4. Cool completely in pan and dust with confectioners' sugar.

Gingerbread Better-Than-Boxed Squares

1¾ cups unbleached all-purpose
  flour

1 teaspoon ground cinnamon

1 teaspoon ground ginger

¼ teaspoon ground cloves

1 teaspoon baking powder

¼ cup vegetable shortening

¾ cup granulated sugar

1¼ teaspoons baking soda

½ cup unsulfured molasses

1 cup boiling water

Confectioners' sugar (to dust)

These are very cakelike. They are absolutely delicious. It is a dark gingerbread and one of my friends says they are super yummy. They go over real big and this is one of her favorites.

1. Preheat oven to 325°F. Lightly butter and dust with flour an 8-inch square baking pan. Tap out excess flour.

2. In a large bowl, combine flour, spices, and baking powder. Set aside.

3. In a small bowl, with a handheld electric mixer set on medium speed, beat shortening and sugar until fluffy. Add baking soda and molasses; stir in the boiling water.

4. Add molasses mixture to flour and, with a wooden spoon, mix until completely smooth.

5. Pour batter into prepared pan and bake for 25 to 30 minutes or until toothpick inserted in center comes out clean.

6. Cool completely in pan approximately 20 minutes before cutting. Dust with confectioners' sugar and serve.

Ginger Squares

2 cups unbleached all-purpose
  flour

½ cup firmly packed brown sugar

½ cup orange marmalade

⅓ cup molasses

½ teaspoon ground cinnamon

½ teaspoon ground ginger

1 teaspoon baking soda

½ cup water

These are perfect for a lunch box—tasty with the look of pudgy cookies.

1. Preheat oven to 350°F. Lightly butter a 15 x 10 x 2-inch pan or two 8 x 8-inch pans.

2. In a large bowl, with a handheld electric mixer set on low speed, combine flour, sugar, marmalade, molasses, cinnamon, ginger, baking soda, and water. Beat until well blended, approximately 3 minutes. Batter will be thick.

3. Spread evenly into pan and bake for 15 minutes of until tooth-pick inserted in center comes out clean.

4. Cool in pan completely before cutting into bars.

Granola Bars

1 cup firmly packed brown sugar

⅓ cup granulated sugar

½ cup butter or margarine, softened

2¼ tablespoons honey

1 teaspoon vanilla extract

1 cup unbleached all-purpose flour

1 teaspoon cornstarch

1 teaspoon ground cinnamon

1 teaspoon baking powder

1½ cups quick rolled oats

1 cup crisp rice cereal

1 cup chopped almonds

1 cup raisins or semisweet chocolate chips

¼ cup wheat germ

These go over very big with children as well as adults. Much better than store-bought granola bars!

1. Preheat oven to 350°F. Lightly butter a 13 x 9 x 2-inch pan.

2. In a large bowl, with a handheld electric mixer set on medium speed, beat sugars and butter or margarine until fluffy; blend in honey and vanilla. Slowly add flour, cornstarch, cinnamon, and baking powder; beat at low speed. With a wooden spoon, fold in oats, rice cereal, almonds, raisins or chocolate chips, and wheat germ until well mixed. Place in prepared pan and bake for 20 minutes until golden brown.

3. Cool completely and serve cut into bars.

Lemon Coconut Bars

BOTTOM LAYER

¾ cup butter or margarine, room temperature

½ cup confectioners' sugar, sifted

1¾ cups unbleached all-purpose flour

1 teaspoon baking powder

⅓ cup water

TOP LAYER

¾ cup granulated sugar

4 tablespoons unbleached all-purpose flour

¼ cup butter or margarine, room temperature

1 teaspoon baking powder

¼ cup lemon juice

½ teaspoon grated lemon rind

½ cup flaked coconut

These are great-tasting lemony cookie bars—thin and delicious.

1. Preheat oven to 350°F. Lightly butter an 8 x 8-inch square pan.

2. *TO PREPARE BOTTOM LAYER:* In a medium bowl, with a pastry blender, cut in butter or margarine, sugar, flour, baking powder, and water until mixture forms a pastrylike crumbly dough.

3. Pat into prepared pan evenly. Bake for 20 minutes. Remove and set aside.

4. *TO PREPARE TOP LAYER:* Meanwhile, in a separate medium bowl, with a wooden spoon, stir together sugar, flour, butter or margarine, baking powder, lemon juice, lemon rind, and coconut.

5. Spread evenly over hot crust, pressing down, and bake for 10 minutes longer until lightly golden brown. Cut into bars when completely cooled.

Melt-in-Your-Mouth Chocolate Kringles

makes 2½ to 3
dozen squares

Vegetable oil cooking spray

1½ cups semisweet chocolate
chips

½ cup mini-marshmallows

¾ cup margarine or butter, room
temperature

¼ cup light corn syrup

2½ teaspoons vanilla extract

1 cup confectioners' sugar

4 cups crisp rice cereal

¼ cup chopped toffee bar, or
crunch mix

Children in particular love these wonderful-tasting bars.

1. Line a 13 x 9 x 2-inch pan with wax paper coated with vegetable oil spray on bottom. Set aside.

2. In a large saucepan, combine chocolate chips, marshmallows, margarine or butter, and corn syrup; stir over low heat until melted. Remove from heat and stir in vanilla, confectioners' sugar, crisp rice cereal, and toffee bar pieces; mix until completely coated.

3. Scrape out chocolate mixture and spread into prepared pan evenly; then place in refrigerator for 2 hours to set. Cut into squares.

Orange Spice Molasses Squares

½ cup vegetable shortening

½ cup granulated sugar

1 (6-ounce) can orange juice
  concentrate, thawed

½ cup quick rolled oats

½ cup molasses

2 cups unbleached all-purpose
  flour

1½ cups baking soda

¼ teaspoon ground ginger

1¼ teaspoons ground cinnamon

½ cup orange soda

½ cup raisins

½ cup nuts, chopped

ORANGE ICING

1½ cups confectioners' sugar

4 teaspoons orange juice

½ cup butter or margarine, room
  temperature

With a taste like an expensive carrot cake, these squares have a rich flavor. Perfect with a cup of coffee.

1. Preheat oven to 325°F. Lightly butter a 13 x 9 x 2-inch pan.

2. In a large bowl, with a handheld electric mixer set on medium speed, beat shortening and sugar until fluffy. Add orange juice, oats, molasses, flour, baking soda, ginger, and cinnamon. Beat for 3 minutes until smooth; with a spoon stir in soda, raisins, and nuts.

3. Pour into prepared pan and bake for 30 to 40 minutes. Cool on wire rack.

4. *TO PREPARE ICING:* In a small pan, combine confectioners' sugar, orange juice, and butter or margarine with a handheld electric mixer set on medium speed, blending ingredients together until smooth.

Pineapple Squares

½ cup butter or margarine, room temperature

¾ cup lightly packed brown sugar

1 teaspoon vanilla extract

1½ cups unbleached all-purpose flour

1 teaspoon baking soda

1 cup well-drained crushed pineapple

TOPPING

¼ cup butter or margarine, melted

1 teaspoon vanilla extract

½ cup granulated sugar

1 cup shredded coconut

One of my favorites. This is a tropical blend that teases your tastebuds.

1. Preheat oven to 375°F. Lightly butter a 9 x 9-inch baking pan.

2. In a large bowl, with a handheld electric mixer set on medium speed, cream butter or margarine and sugar; add vanilla. Slowly add flour and baking soda and mix thoroughly. Press batter evenly into prepared pan and bake for 15 minutes.

3. Remove from oven and cool for 5 minutes in pan on wire rack. Spread pineapple evenly over baked crust. Set aside.

4. *TO PREPARE TOPPING:* Meanwhile, in a small bowl, combine melted butter or margarine, vanilla, sugar, and coconut; with a spoon, stir until blended.

5. Spread evenly over pineapple and return pan to oven. Bake another 30 minutes until topping appears lightly browned.

Delicious, Easy Pumpkin Bars

¼ cup cornstarch

2 cups canned pumpkin

2 cups mini-marshmallows

¾ cup firmly packed brown sugar

1 (1-ounce) packet unflavored
  gelatin

1 teaspoon ground cinnamon

¼ teaspoon ground nutmeg

¼ teaspoon ground ginger

CRUST

½ cup butter or margarine,
  melted

1¼ cups crushed graham cracker
  crumbs

TOPPING

Whipped cream (optional)

Bring these to a party—they always go over with a bang.

1. Preheat oven to 350°F.

2. In a large bowl, with a wooden spoon, stir cornstarch, pumpkin, 1 cup mini-marshmallows, brown sugar, gelatin, cinnamon, nutmeg, and ginger until smooth, making sure cornstarch has no lumps. Set aside.

3. *TO PREPARE CRUST:* Place butter or margarine in a microwave-safe bowl, and microwave on high setting for 1 minute until butter melts; stir in graham cracker crumbs until moist.

4. Pat crust into an 8 x 8 x 2-inch baking dish. Top with remaining 1 cup mini-marshmallows and place in oven for 5 minutes until marshmallows melt; remove from oven and spread evenly.

5. Spread pumpkin mixture over melted marshmallows and bake for 30 minutes. Remove from oven and cool completely.

6. Cover with plastic wrap and refrigerate for several hours or overnight until set. Then cut with a sharp knife.

7. Serve with whipped cream topping if used.

Heavenly Brownies

¾ cup unsweetened cocoa
   powder

1¾ cups sugar

1¾ cups unbleached all-purpose
   flour

⅓ cup vegetable oil

1 cup non-fat sour cream

¼ cup corn syrup

2 teaspoons white vinegar

1 teaspoon vanilla extract

1 teaspoon baking soda

½ cup chocolate chips

½ cup chopped walnuts (optional)

A perfect brownie, without eggs. You never would have thought anyone could have pulled this off.

1. Preheat oven to 350°F. Lightly butter a 9 x 2 x 13-inch pan.

2. In a large bowl, combine cocoa, sugar, flour, oil, sour cream, corn syrup, vinegar, vanilla, and baking soda. With a handheld electric mixer set on medium speed, beat ingredients until smooth, approximately 3 minutes. With a wooden spoon, fold in chocolate chips and chopped walnuts (if used).

3. Pour batter into prepared pan evenly and bake for 20 minutes. Cool in pan on wire rack for 30 minutes. Cut with a sharp knife.

Variation

For a little sweeter brownie you may add ⅓ cup corn syrup instead of ¼ cup.

Chocolate Caramel Candy Brownies

makes 16 brownies

¾ cup unsweetened cocoa
   powder

1½ cups sugar

1¾ cups unbleached all-purpose
   flour

½ cup non-fat sour cream

½ cup skim milk

⅓ cup vegetable oil

⅓ cup corn syrup

2 teaspoons vinegar

1 teaspoon baking soda

1 teaspoon vanilla extract

½ cup chocolate chips

TOPPING

1 (9-ounce) package individually
   wrapped chocolate caramel
   candy pieces

1 tablespoon milk

½ cup chopped nuts (your choice)

A kids' favorite—they love the combination of caramel and chocolate.

1. Preheat oven to 350°F. Lightly butter a 9 x 13-inch pan.

2. In a large bowl, with a handheld electric mixer set on medium speed, blend in cocoa, sugar, flour, sour cream, milk, oil, corn syrup, vinegar, baking soda, and vanilla until smooth. With a wooden spoon, fold in chocolate chips.

3. Pour into prepared pan and bake for 20 minutes.

4. *TO PREPARE TOPPING:* Meanwhile, in a medium saucepan, combine chocolate caramel candy and milk and melt over low heat, stirring constantly. Or place candy in a microwave-safe bowl, and microwave on high setting for 1 minute; remove and stir until melted. Spread over warm brownies and sprinkle with nuts. Place pan on a wire rack to cool completely before cutting.

No Cow Brownies

Vegetable oil cooking spray

1¾ cups unbleached all-purpose flour

½ cup cocoa powder

1 cup sugar

1½ teaspoons baking soda

¼ cup vegetable oil

½ cup water

⅓ cup light corn syrup

1 teaspoon vanilla extract

1½ teaspoons white vinegar

½ cup semisweet chocolate chips

½ cup chopped walnuts (optional)

Chewy and great-tasting. A friend of mine who is allergic to both eggs and milk loves these. You will too.

1. Preheat oven to 350°F. Lightly spray an 8 x 8-inch pan with vegetable spray.

2. In a medium bowl, combine flour, cocoa, sugar, baking soda, oil, water, corn syrup, vanilla, vinegar, and chocolate chips; stir with a wooden spoon, batter will be thick. Fold in nuts (if used).

3. Spoon evenly into prepared pan and bake for 20 to 25 minutes (brownies will come away from sides of pan when done). Cool completely on a wire rack before cutting.

Perfect Moist Applesauce Brownies

3 (1-ounce) squares unsweetened baking chocolate

½ cup butter or margarine, room temperature

¼ cup vegetable oil

2 tablespoons light corn syrup

¼ cup water

2 teaspoons vinegar

2 teaspoons vanilla extract

1 cup sweetened applesauce

2 cups unbleached all-purpose flour

2 cups sugar

1 teaspoon baking powder

1 teaspoon baking soda

½ cup semisweet chocolate chips

1 cup chopped walnuts

These are very rich and delicious. They are chewy just as a nice brownie should be.

1. Preheat oven to 350°F. Lightly butter a 13 x 9 x 2-inch pan.

2. Put chocolate and butter or margarine in a medium microwave-safe bowl, and microwave for 1 minute on high setting or until melted; remove and stir in oil, corn syrup, water, vinegar, vanilla, and applesauce. Set aside.

3. In a large bowl, combine flour, sugar, baking powder, and baking soda; with a wooden spoon, stir until completely mixed. Pour in melted chocolate mixture and stir until smooth; fold in chocolate chips and nuts.

4. Spread batter into prepared pan and bake for 25 to 30 minutes. Completely cool in pan on wire rack for 30 minutes. Cut with a sharp knife and remove onto a serving plate.

NOTE: For a more cakelike brownie use only ¾ cup applesauce.

Muffins, Rolls, and Scones

Applesauce Muffins

1 cup quick rolled oats or oat bran
  cereal

1¼ cups all-purpose unbleached
  flour

¾ cup granulated sugar

2 teaspoons baking powder

¼ cup raisins

1 cup unsweetened applesauce

1 teaspoon vanilla extract

1 teaspoon grated lemon peel
  (optional)

4 tablespoons milk

¼ cup vegetable oil

TOPPING

1½ tablespoons brown sugar

½ teaspoon ground cinnamon

¼ cup ground almonds

These are a great lunch box or breakfast snack.

1. Preheat oven to 400°F. Lightly butter twelve 3 x 1¼-inch (3½-
to 4-ounce) muffin cups.

2. In a large bowl, combine oats or cereal, flour, sugar, baking
powder, raisins, applesauce, vanilla, lemon peel (if used), milk,
and vegetable oil; with a wooden spoon, stir until completely
mixed.

3. Spoon batter into prepared muffin cups, filling three-quarters
full.

4. *TO PREPARE TOPPING:* In a small bowl, combine sugar, cinnamon, and ground almonds; stir with spoon. Sprinkle each muffin
evenly with topping before baking.

5. Bake 15 minutes or until toothpick inserted in center comes
out clean. Cool on wire racks 15 minutes before removing from
pan.

Apple Dapple Cinnamon Oat Bran Muffins

makes 1 dozen muffins

1¼ cups oat bran cereal

1¼ cups unbleached all-purpose flour

⅓ cup firmly packed light brown sugar

1 tablespoon baking powder

1 teaspoon baking soda

¼ teaspoon ground cinnamon

1¼ cups apple juice

¼ cup margarine or butter, room temperature

1 teaspoon vanilla extract

1 cup seedless raisins

1 apple, peeled, cored and chopped

1¼ cups nuts (optional)

These are very nutritious and perfect for the lunch box.

1. Preheat oven to 375°F. Lightly butter twelve 3 x 1¼-inch (3½- to 4-ounce) muffin cups.

2. In a large bowl, combine cereal, flour, brown sugar, baking powder, baking soda, and cinnamon. With a wooden spoon, stir so they are mixed; stir in apple juice, margarine or butter, vanilla, raisins, chopped apple, nuts (if used) until completely mixed and moistened.

3. Spoon batter into prepared muffin cups, filling three-quarters full, and bake for 25 to 30 minutes or until golden.

Apple Oaty Muffins

2⅓ cups oat bran cereal

2 teaspoons baking powder

¾ cup honey

½ cup water

1¼ cups applesauce

½ cup raisins

½ cup nuts (optional)

1 teaspoon grated lemon peel
  (optional)

These are truly moist and delicious.

1. Preheat oven to 400°F. Lightly butter twelve 3 x 1¼-inch (3½- to 4-ounce) muffin cups.

2. In a large bowl, combine cereal, baking powder, honey, and water; mix until moistened. (If batter is too dry, add a little more water to it.) Add applesauce and raisins and stir in nuts (if used) and lemon peel (if used) until combined. Fill prepared muffin cups almost full.

3. Bake for 15 to 20 minutes until golden brown.

Banana Muffins

1 cup mashed ripe bananas
  (approximately 2)

2 cups unbleached all-purpose
  flour

3 tablespoons vegetable oil

1 cup sugar

1 tablespoon baking powder

1½ teaspoons baking soda

½ cup apple juice

1 teaspoon vanilla extract

½ cup chopped walnuts

These banana muffins have a great old-fashioned taste.

1. Preheat oven to 350°F. Lightly butter twelve 3 x 1¼-inch (3½- to 4-ounce) muffin cups.

2. In a large bowl, with a wooden spoon, combine mashed bananas, flour, oil, sugar, baking powder, baking soda, apple juice, vanilla, and nuts; stir vigorously until completely blended.

3. Spoon batter into prepared muffin cups, filling three-quarters full, and bake for 15 to 20 minutes until golden brown.

Banana Orange Nut Muffins

makes 1 dozen muffins

2¼ cups unbleached all-purpose flour

1 cup sugar

2 teaspoons baking powder

1 teaspoon baking soda

¼ cup vegetable oil

1 cup orange juice

2 bananas, mashed

½ cup nuts, finely chopped (optional)

Orange juice provides an extra special zip. A delicious combination of flavors.

1. Preheat oven to 400°F. Lightly butter twelve 3 x 1¼-inch (3½- to 4-ounce) muffin cups.

2. In a large bowl, combine flour, sugar, baking powder, and baking soda; with a wooden spoon, stir until dry ingredients are mixed. Stir in oil, orange juice, mashed bananas, and nuts (if used) until smooth.

3. Spoon prepared muffin batter into cups, filling half full, and bake for 20 to 25 minutes or until browned on top.

4. Remove and cool in pan on wire rack.

Banana Bran Muffins

1 cup bran or bran cereal

1 cup unbleached all-purpose
  flour

¼ cup sugar

1 tablespoon baking powder

1 teaspoon ground cinnamon

1 cup mashed ripe bananas

½ cup buttermilk

3 tablespoons vegetable oil

1 cup raisins

These are also a lunch box muffin and a healthy snack.

1. Preheat oven to 375°F. Lightly butter eight 3 x 1¼-inch (3½- to 4-ounce) muffin cups.

2. In a large bowl, combine bran or bran cereal, flour, sugar, baking powder, and cinnamon; with a wooden spoon, stir until mixed. Set aside.

3. In a small bowl, combine bananas, buttermilk, oil, and raisins until completely mixed. Pour banana mixture into dry mixture all at once and stir until moist (add a little more milk if necessary).

4. Spoon batter into prepared muffin cups, filling half full.

5. Bake for 20 to 25 minutes or until toothpick inserted in center comes out clean.

6. Cool on wire rack in pan.

Bran (Perfect) Muffins

1½ cups skim milk

2½ cups unprocessed bran

1½ cups unbleached all-purpose
  flour

1 teaspoon baking powder

½ teaspoon baking soda

¾ cup sugar

⅓ cup vegetable oil

¾ cup water

These are perfect for breakfast and healthy too! They taste like muffins you would find in a bakery—only better.

1. Preheat oven to 375°F. Lightly butter bottoms only of twelve 3 x 1¼-inch (3½- to 4-ounce) muffin cups or line with paper baking cups.

2. In a large bowl, combine milk and bran; let stand for 3 minutes. Then, with a wooden spoon, stir in flour, baking powder, baking soda, sugar, oil, and water until completely combined.

3. Spoon batter into prepared muffin cups, filling three-quarters full.

4. Bake for 20 minutes, or until golden brown.

Joyce's Blueberry Muffins

2 cups plus 2 tablespoons
  unbleached all-purpose flour

½ cup granulated sugar

3 teaspoons baking powder

1 teaspoon baking soda

1 teaspoon grated lemon peel

1 tablespoon lemon juice

1 cup light cream or milk

½ cup applesauce

1 cup drained fresh or frozen
  blueberries

TOPPING

3 tablespoons brown sugar

1 tablespoon margarine or butter,
  room temperature

¼ teaspoon ground cinnamon

¼ teaspoon ground nutmeg

⅓ cup nuts, finely chopped

My friend Joyce is an excellent baker who loves to make everything fresh. Her recipes are wonderful—always come out well, even when I adapt them for egg-free bakers.

1. Preheat oven to 375°F. Lightly butter twelve 3 x 1¼-inch (3½- to 4-ounce) muffin cups.

2. In a large bowl, combine 2 cups flour, sugar, baking powder, baking soda, lemon peel and juice, milk, and applesauce; with a wooden spoon, mix until thoroughly combined.

3. In a small bowl, toss blueberries with remaining 2 tablespoons flour just to coat (this prevents them from sinking), then fold them into batter gently. Spoon batter into prepared muffin cups, filling half full. Set aside.

4. *TO PREPARE TOPPING:* In a separate small bowl, with a fork, stir sugar, margarine or butter, cinnamon, nutmeg, and nuts until crumbly. Spoon evenly on each muffin before baking.

5. Bake for 15 to 20 minutes or until light golden brown. Serve warm.

Corn Muffins

1 cup self-rising cornmeal

1 cup unbleached all-purpose
flour

1 teaspoon baking powder

¼ cup honey

2 tablespoons sugar

¼ cup vegetable oil

2 tablespoons margarine, room
temperature

¾ cup skim milk

1 tablespoon vinegar

¼ cup club soda

Corn muffins are an old-fashioned favorite. Now you can have your muffin and eat it too!

1. Preheat oven to 375°F. Lightly butter twelve 3 x 1¼-inch (3½- to 4-ounce) muffin cups.

2. In a large bowl, with a handheld electric mixer set on low speed, beat cornmeal, flour, baking powder, honey, sugar, oil, margarine, milk, vinegar, and club soda until completely smooth (approximately 3 minutes).

3. Spoon batter into prepared muffin cups, filling three-quarters full.

4. Bake for 20 minutes or until golden brown.

Sour Cream Corn Muffins

makes 1 dozen muffins

1¼ cups stone-ground cornmeal

1¼ cups unbleached all-purpose
  flour, sifted

½ cup sugar

1½ tablespoons baking powder

1 cup skim milk

1 tablespoon white vinegar

½ cup sour cream

1 teaspoon vanilla extract

These are a great variation with a subtle, irresistible flavor. People really love them.

1. Preheat oven to 375°F. Lightly butter twelve 3 x 1¼-inch (3½- to 4-ounce) muffin cups.

2. In a large mixing bowl, combine cornmeal, flour, sugar, and baking powder; with a wooden spoon, stir until mixed. Stir in milk, vinegar, sour cream, and vanilla until well blended.

3. Spoon batter into prepared muffin cups, filling three-quarters full.

4. Bake for 15 to 20 minutes or until golden brown.

5. Cool on a wire rack for 20 minutes before serving.

Variation

Add ½ cup drained canned corn after sour cream and vanilla and fold in.

Kathleen's Miniature Coffee Muffin Cakes

makes 1 dozen muffin cakes

1¾ cups unbleached all-purpose
   flour

1 tablespoon baking powder

1 teaspoon baking soda

1 teaspoon ground cinnamon

1 (3⅝-ounce) package instant
   vanilla pudding

¼ cup granulated sugar

⅓ cup margarine, room
   temperature

1 tablespoon vegetable oil

1 teaspoon vanilla extract

1¼ cups skim milk

¾ cup water

WALNUT TOPPING

½ cup chopped walnuts

⅓ cup firmly packed light brown
   sugar

1 tablespoon margarine, melted

½ teaspoon ground cinnamon

These delicious muffins are great for snacks. The crumb topping has a taste children just love. This is definitely one for the lunch box.

1. Preheat oven to 375°F. Lightly butter twelve 3 x 1¼-inch (3½- to 4-ounce) muffin cups.

2. In a large bowl, combine flour, baking powder, baking soda, cinnamon, pudding, sugar, margarine, and oil; with a wooden spoon, stir until mixed. With a handheld electric mixer set on medium speed, beat in vanilla, milk, and water until smooth. Spoon batter into prepared muffin cups, filling two-thirds full. Set aside.

3. *TO PREPARE TOPPING:* In a small bowl, mix walnuts, sugar, melted margarine, and cinnamon.

4. Spoon on walnut topping evenly, pressing down slightly into batter so nuts stay on.

5. Bake 20 minutes or until toothpick inserted in center comes out clean. Remove from oven and cool in pan on wire rack until completely cooled.

Cinnamon Honey Muffins

makes 1 dozen muffins

¾ cup bran

1 cup low-fat milk

1 tablespoon lemon juice

½ cup honey

½ cup vegetable oil

½ cup raisins

½ cup grated carrots

1¼ cups unbleached all-purpose
  flour, sifted

2 teaspoons baking soda

1 teaspoon ground nutmeg or
  ground cinnamon

This muffin is especially chock full of carrots and good for you. I suggest making a bunch and freezing them.

1. Preheat oven to 400°F. Lightly butter twelve 3 x 1¼-inch (3½- to 4-ounce) muffin cups.

2. In a large bowl, combine bran, milk, lemon juice, honey, oil, raisins, and carrots; let stand 5 minutes.

3. With a wooden spoon, stir in flour, baking soda, and nutmeg or cinnamon until completely combined.

4. Spoon batter into prepared muffin cups, filling three-quarters full, and bake for 15 to 20 minutes or until tester inserted in center comes out clean.

Lemon Muffins

1½ tablespoons grated lemon rind

1 medium lemon, squeezed

2 cups unbleached all-purpose flour

1 heaping teaspoon baking powder

1 teaspoon baking soda

¾ cup sugar

½ cup water

½ cup low-fat lemon yogurt or low-fat sour cream

4 teaspoons oil

If you love lemons, you will be absolutely dazzled by the taste of these muffins.

1. Preheat oven to 375°F. Lightly butter twelve 3 x 1¼-inch (3½- to 4-ounce) muffin cups.

2. In a large bowl, combine lemon rind, lemon juice, flour, baking powder, baking soda, sugar, water, lemon yogurt or sour cream, and oil. With a wooden spoon, stir until combined (batter will be a little thick but moist).

3. Spoon out batter into prepared muffin cups, filling half full. Bake 15 to 20 minutes.

4. Cool on wire rack in pan for 10 minutes before removing.

Variations

Add 1 tablespoon of poppy seeds to batter and/or ½ cup nuts or ½ cup dry blueberries.

Substitute same amount of orange juice and orange yogurt in place of lemons.

Loaded With Jam Muffins

makes 1 dozen muffins

1½ cups whole-wheat flour

3 tablespoons sugar

½ teaspoon salt

1 teaspoon baking soda

1 cup buttermilk

3 tablespoons vegetable oil

12 teaspoons jelly or jam

These have jam in them already. Nothing else to do to them except sit back and enjoy!

1. Preheat oven to 400°F. Lightly butter twelve 3 x 1¼-inch (3½- to 4-ounce) muffin cups.

2. In a large bowl, with a wooden spoon, combine flour, sugar, salt, baking soda, buttermilk, and oil. Stir just until dry ingredients are moistened.

3. Spoon batter into prepared muffin cups, filling about one third full. Place 1 teaspoon jelly or jam in the center of each, then top with remaining batter, filling each cup about two-thirds full.

4. Bake for 20 to 25 minutes or until done. Remove immediately from muffin cups. Serve hot.

Good Morning Muffins

2 cups unbleached all-purpose flour

1¼ cups granulated sugar

1 teaspoon baking soda

2 teaspoons baking powder

1 teaspoon ground cinnamon

1½ cups shredded carrots

1½ cups applesauce

¼ cup vegetable oil

½ cup flaked coconut

1 teaspoon vanilla extract

⅓ cup finely chopped pecans

Perfect with a cup of coffee. Moist and delicious!

1. Preheat oven to 375°F. Line twelve 3 x 1¼-inch (3½- to 4-ounce) muffin cups with paper baking cups.

2. In a mixing bowl, combine flour, sugar, baking soda, baking powder, and cinnamon; with wooden spoon, stir until mixed. Stir in shredded carrots, applesauce, oil, coconut, and vanilla until completely combined. Fold in pecans.

3. Spoon batter into prepared muffin cups, filling to the top. Bake for 20 to 25 minutes or until golden brown.

4. Remove from pans and cool on a wire rack; serve warm or cold.

Pear Muffins

makes 1 dozen muffins

2 cups unbleached all-purpose
 flour, sifted

1 teaspoon baking powder

1 teaspoon baking soda

½ teaspoon ground cinnamon

¼ teaspoon allspice

½ cup sugar

¼ cup vegetable oil

½ cup plain low-fat yogurt

½ cup skim milk

1 cup peeled chopped ripe pears

½ teaspoon almond extract

These have an unusual taste. They also make a great healthy and wholesome kids' snack.

1. Preheat oven to 375°F. Lightly butter 12-cup 3 x 1¼-inch (3½- to 4-ounce) muffin pan.

2. In a large bowl, with a wooden spoon, stir in flour, baking powder, baking soda, cinnamon, allspice, and sugar; stir until well combined. Stir in oil, yogurt, milk, pears, and extract.

3. Spoon batter into prepared muffin cups, filling each cup two-thirds full. Bake for 20 to 25 minutes or until toothpick inserted in center comes out clean. Serve warm.

Peach Muffins

2 cups unbleached all-purpose
   flour

1 tablespoon baking powder

1 teaspoon baking soda

¼ teaspoon allspice

¼ cup firmly packed dark brown
   sugar

¼ cup vegetable oil

1 cup no-fat sour cream or yogurt

⅔ cup fresh or canned peaches,
   drained and chopped

These muffins are great with tea. They have a delicious, interesting flavor.

1. Preheat oven to 400°F. Lightly butter twelve 3 x 1¼-inch (3½- to 4-ounce) muffin cups.

2. In a large bowl, with a wooden spoon, stir flour, baking powder, baking soda, allspice, sugar, oil, and sour cream or yogurt; stir ingredients just until mixed. Fold in peaches gently (batter will be lumpy).

3. Spoon batter into prepared muffin cups, filling three-quarters full.

4. Bake 20 minutes or until golden brown.

Yogurt Muffins

2½ cups unbleached all-purpose flour

¼ cup sugar

½ cup quick rolled oats

4 teaspoons baking powder

2 teaspoons baking soda

⅔ cup vegetable shortening

2 tablespoons oil

2 cups low-fat lemon yogurt

These are simple to make and very light, almost like a popover, with a mild lemon flavor.

1. Preheat oven to 375°F. Line twelve 3 x 1¼-inch (3½- to 4-ounce) muffin cups with paper liners.

2. In a large bowl, with a handheld electric mixer set on medium speed, beat flour, sugar, oats, baking powder, baking soda, shortening, oil, and yogurt all at once. Mix approximately 3 minutes until completely combined.

3. Spoon batter into prepared muffin cups, filling two-thirds full.

4. Bake for 25 to 35 minutes.

Perfect Caramel Rolls

DOUGH

2 cups unbleached all-purpose
  flour

1 cup whole-wheat flour

¼ cup granulated sugar

1 (¼-ounce) package active dry
  yeast

¾ cup milk

⅓ cup water

2 tablespoons vegetable
  shortening

FILLING

1 cup firmly packed brown sugar

⅓ cup butter or margarine,
  melted

¾ cup chopped nuts

1 tablespoon grated orange peel

1 teaspoon vanilla extract

1 tablespoon honey

These have a great, rich flavor. They are a sweet brunch or breakfast roll that can also be enjoyed as dessert. You will need to make the dough in advance.

1. *TO PREPARE DOUGH:* In a large bowl, combine ½ cup unbleached all-purpose flour, whole-wheat flour, sugar, and yeast; blend well. Set aside. In a small saucepan, heat milk, water, and shortening until warm. Add warm mixture to flour mixture.

2. With a wooden spoon, stir ingredients together, adding ½ cup at a time remaining flour and more water if needed to form a stiff dough. Then turn out onto a floured surface and knead for 5 to 8 minutes until dough is smooth.

3. Lightly oil a large bowl, place smooth dough in bowl, cover with plastic wrap and a towel.

4. Let rise in a warm, draft-free area until double in size, approximately 1 to 1½ hours.

5. Lightly butter a 9-inch square pan. Set aside.

6. Punch dough down several times to remove air bubbles after it has risen.

7. Roll out dough to a 16 x 12-inch rectangle on a lightly floured surface. Set aside.

8. *TO PREPARE FILLING:* In a medium bowl, combine brown sugar, melted butter or margarine, chopped nuts, grated orange peel, vanilla, and honey. With a fork, mix thoroughly.

9. Spread mixture evenly over dough; then, starting with 16-inch side, roll dough tightly; pinch edges to seal dough.

10. Cut 1-inch-thick slices; place them in prepared pan cut side down. Cover and let rise again until double in size, approximately 1 hour.

11. Preheat oven to 350°F. Uncover pan and bake for 30 minutes or until golden brown.

Special Fan Rolls

3½ cups unbleached all-purpose
    flour

1½ (¼-ounce) packages yeast

1¼ cups milk

¼ cup granulated sugar

½ cup vegetable shortening

3 teaspoons vegetable oil

¼ teaspoon nutmeg

¼ teaspoon salt

⅓ cup water (to seal dough)

FILLING

2 tablespoons light corn syrup

½ cup firmly packed light brown
    sugar

¾ teaspoon grated lemon peel

1 cup raisins

1¼ teaspoons ground cinnamon

1 tablespoon butter, softened

Milk (just to brush tops)

ICING

1¼ cups sifted confectioners'
    sugar

4 tablespoons milk

These are great for impressing your guests, at the holidays or at any special gathering. Definitely sweet as an after-dinner roll, or at breakfast, or simply with coffee. They come out looking very pretty.

1. In a medium bowl, combine half of flour and package of yeast. Set aside.

2. In a small saucepan, heat on low setting milk, granulated sugar, shortening, oil, nutmeg, and salt just until shortening starts to melt. Add to flour mixture. With a handheld electric mixer set on low speed, beat, scraping sides of bowl; stir in remaining flour (dough will be soft). Cut dough into 4 quarters. Shape each into a disk. Coat each quarter with oil and wrap each in plastic wrap. Chill in refrigerator overnight.

3. After dough has chilled, take out one of the quarters and let stand at room temperature for 10 minutes. On a lightly floured surface, roll out dough with a rolling pin to 12 x 8-inch rectangle.

4. Cut rectangle into six 4-inch squares.

5. *TO PREPARE FILLING:* In a small bowl, combine corn syrup, brown sugar, lemon peel, raisins, cinnamon, and butter. With a spoon, stir just to mix; set aside.

6. On half of each square spread 1 tablespoon of filling to within ½ inch of the edges.

7. Moisten edges with your finger dipped in water. Fold square in half.

8. Line 2 baking sheets with foil and lightly butter them. Place dough rectangles onto prepared baking sheets, spacing them 3 inches apart. Cut 4 crosswise slashes in each square three-quarters through the dough to form fan shape. Spread slashes apart, forming a curve or coxcomb shape. Cover with a towel and allow dough curves to rise in a warm place, until they are double in size (approximately 1 hour).

9. Preheat oven to 375°F.

10. Remove towel and brush tops with milk. Place pans in oven on center rack; bake for 15 to 20 minutes or until golden.

11. *TO PREPARE ICING:* Into a small bowl, sift confectioners' sugar. Add milk and stir until smooth and creamy, adding a little more milk if necessary for drizzle consistency. Drizzle over each roll and serve.

Lemon Nut Rolls

makes 16 rolls

DOUGH

3½ cups unbleached all-purpose
   flour

⅓ cup mashed potato flakes

⅓ cup granulated sugar

¼ teaspoon salt

1 teaspoon grated lemon peel

1 (¼-ounce) package active dry
   yeast

¾ cup warm water

½ cup warm milk

⅓ cup melted margarine or butter

3 tablespoons lemon juice

2 tablespoons vegetable oil

FILLING

2 tablespoons margarine or
   butter, softened

¾ cup granulated sugar

½ cup chopped pecans

1½ teaspoons grated lemon peel

1 tablespoon poppy seeds
   (optional)

GLAZE

1 cup confectioners' sugar

2 teaspoons grated lemon peel

1 teaspoon lemon juice

2 tablespoons cream or milk

What a roll! This one you'll have to taste for yourself. You will not be disappointed. I serve them after dinner but they are great for brunch too.

1. *TO PREPARE DOUGH:* In a large bowl, with a wooden spoon, combine flour, potato flakes, sugar, salt, lemon peel, yeast, water, milk, melted margarine or butter, lemon juice, and oil. Stir for 3 to 5 minutes, adding more flour if necessary, until the mixture forms a stiff dough. Cover with plastic wrap and place in a warm place to rise until double in bulk, at least 1 hour.

2. Lightly butter and dust with flour two 9-inch round pans. Tap out extra flour. Set aside.

3. On a floured surface, turn dough out and knead and flour until dough is no longer sticky. Roll dough out to a 16 x 12-inch rectangle. Spread with filling ingredients, first spreading dough with margarine or butter, then sprinkling evenly with sugar, pecans, lemon peel, and poppy seeds (if used).

4. Starting with 16-inch side, roll up in a jelly roll fashion tightly; pinch edges to seal. Then cut into sixteen 1-inch slices.

5. Place slices cut side down in prepared pans, 3 inches apart; cover with towels, and let rise once more in a warm place until double in size, approximately 1 hour.

6. Preheat oven to 350°F. Uncover pans and bake for 30 minutes or until light golden brown.

7. *TO PREPARE GLAZE:* In a small bowl, stir confectioners' sugar, lemon peel, lemon juice, and cream or milk until smooth, and drizzle over rolls while they are warm. If you desire a thinner consistency, keep adding cream or milk a little at a time until it is right consistency.

Irish Scones

2½ cups unbleached all-purpose
  flour
½ cup sugar
2½ teaspoons baking powder
2½ teaspoons caraway seeds
¾ cup buttermilk
½ cup currants

These are easy to make and wonderful at teatime. Don't forget the butter and jam when serving.

1. Preheat oven to 375°F. Lightly butter a large cookie sheet.

2. In a large bowl, with a wooden spoon, stir flour, sugar, baking powder, and caraway seeds until blended; slowly add buttermilk just to blend until dough forms (if too sticky, add more flour). Fold in currants.

3. Turn out dough onto a lightly floured surface and with a rolling pin roll out a small circle of dough 1 inch thick. With a (floured) glass or cookie cutter 2 inches in diameter, cut out scones.

4. Repeat and reroll remaining dough until all dough is used.

5. Place scones 2 inches apart on prepared cookie sheet. Bake for 15 minutes or until lightly browned.

Lemon Poppy Seed Scones

1¼ cups buttermilk

2 tablespoons baking powder

2¾ cups unbleached all-purpose
flour

1 tablespoon poppy seeds

1 tablespoon grated lemon rind

1 tablespoon lemon juice

3 tablespoons sugar

Soft and fluffy. A little different from traditional scones.

1. Preheat oven to 400°F. Lightly butter baking sheet.

2. In a large bowl, stir a little buttermilk with baking powder just to blend. Slowly add remaining buttermilk, flour, poppy seeds, lemon rind, lemon juice, and sugar until mixture forms a dough (add a little more flour if it is too sticky).

3. Turn out dough onto a floured surface and shape into a long log 2 inches around. Cut into 1-inch-thick slices. Place on prepared baking sheet.

4. Bake for 15 minutes until lightly browned.

Delicious Dried-Cherry Scones

makes 8 to 10 scones

2 cups unbleached all-purpose
flour

⅓ cup sugar plus 1 tablespoon to
sprinkle on top

1 tablespoon baking powder

1 teaspoon baking soda

½ cup chilled butter, cut up

½ cup buttermilk

1¼ teaspoons vanilla extract

¾ cup dried tart cherries

1 cup chopped almonds or
walnuts

These scones are so scrumptious! This is a great basic scone recipe that can have many different variations such as those listed below—just change the fruit.

1. In a large bowl, combine flour, ⅓ cup sugar, baking powder, baking soda, butter, buttermilk, and vanilla; with a fork, blend until mixture forms a dough, then fold in cherries and chopped nuts.

2. Preheat oven to 400°F. Lightly butter a cookie sheet.

3. Shape into 8 x 2-inch-long log and cut into 8 or 10 pieces. Place on prepared cookie sheet approximately 2 inches apart (they will spread). Sprinkle each evenly with remaining sugar for a frosted top.

4. Place in oven and bake for 12 to 15 minutes (they will be lightly browned on bottom).

5. Cool in pan for a few minutes, then remove to wire rack.

Variations

1 cup whole-wheat flour can be substituted for one of the 2 cups of unbleached flour.

To make a variety of flavors substitute for dried cherries:
1 cup cranberry/orange relish
Grated peel of 1 lemon plus juice

Creamy Piña Colada Scones

2¾ cups unbleached all-purpose
   flour
½ cup sugar
¾ cup shredded coconut
1 tablespoon vanilla extract
1 tablespoon baking powder
1 teaspoon baking soda
¼ cup vegetable shortening
½ cup light sour cream
¼ cup light cream or milk
½ cup drained crushed pineapple
2 teaspoons rum
½ cup chopped walnuts (optional)

British teatime meets Caribbean cocktail hour with this fun, delicious recipe. It's sure to satisfy both purists and fans of something new.

1. Preheat oven to 375°F. Lightly dust a cookie sheet with flour. Tap out excess flour.

2. In a large bowl, with a fork, mix flour, sugar, coconut, vanilla, baking powder, baking soda, vegetable shortening, sour cream, cream or milk, pineapple, rum, and walnuts (if used); mix until a dough forms. (Dough will be a little sticky.)

3. Drop by rounded tablespoons 2 inches apart on prepared cookie sheet.

4. Bake for 15 to 20 minutes until golden brown. Remove from pan immediately onto wire racks to cool.

Pies, Cobblers, Doughnuts, and Strudels

Apple Crumb Pie

makes 1 (9-inch) pie

This is a great apple crumb pie. My daughter loves pies; however, the stores always manage to add eggs.

FILLING

⅔ cup granulated sugar

2½ tablespoons unbleached all-purpose flour

½ teaspoon ground cinnamon

¼ teaspoon ground nutmeg

4 cups peeled, cored, and sliced apples

1 unbaked deep-dish 9-inch piecrust (your choice)

CRUMB TOPPING

½ cup unbleached all-purpose flour

1 teaspoon baking powder

¼ cup butter or margarine

¼ cup firmly packed brown sugar

Whipped topping

1. Preheat oven to 400°F.

2. *TO PREPARE FILLING:* In a large bowl, combine sugar, flour, cinnamon, and nutmeg; mix well. Slowly add apple slices and mix until apples are evenly coated.

3. With a spatula, scrape out apples into an unbaked piecrust shell (your choice).

4. *TO PREPARE CRUMB TOPPING:* In a small bowl, combine flour and baking powder with a pastry blender; cut in butter or margarine and brown sugar until crumbly.

5. Sprinkle topping over apples.

6. Place pie on baking sheet and bake for 35 to 40 minutes until light golden brown color.

7. Allow to cool on wire rack.

8. Top with your favorite whipped topping.

Coffee Cream Pie

1½ cups chocolate cookie crumbs

½ cup butter or margarine, melted

¼ cup mini-chocolate chips

1¼ cups whipping cream

⅔ cup sweetened condensed milk

¼ cup cold coffee

2 teaspoons coffee liqueur

1 teaspoon vanilla extract

1½ cups chopped toffee bar

½ cup chopped nuts

This is a fun frozen dessert that is sort of like ice cream. Kids love to help prepare this (and of course help eat it too).

1. In a small bowl, mix chocolate cookie crumbs and melted butter or margarine; press firmly into a 9-inch pie plate. Sprinkle over mini-chocolate chips evenly. Set aside.

2. Meanwhile, in a large bowl, with a handheld electric mixer set on medium speed, beat for 3 minutes whipping cream, condensed milk, coffee, coffee liqueur, and vanilla just until creamy. Fold in chopped toffee.

3. Pour into pie plate over cookie crumbs and mini-chocolate chips. Sprinkle top with chopped nuts.

4. Place in the freezer overnight. Thaw in refrigerator 2 hours before serving.

Pumpkin Pristine Pie

makes 1 (9-inch) pie

PIECRUST

1½ cups unbleached all-purpose
flour

¼ teaspoon salt

½ cup vegetable shortening

4 tablespoons cold water

FILLING

1 teaspoon vanilla extract

¼ cup brown sugar

2 tablespoons cornstarch

1 teaspoon pumpkin pie spice mix
(or your own)

1 (16-ounce) can pumpkin (2
cups)

1 (14-ounce) can sweetened
condensed milk

Delicious, with a great consistency. Once refrigerated, it really gets solid.

1. Preheat oven to 375°F. Set aside a 9-inch pie plate.

2. *TO PREPARE PIECRUST:* In a medium bowl, combine flour, salt, and shortening; with a pastry blender, cut in until mixture resembles course crumbs. Add water a little at a time and, with a fork, stir gently. When mixture is moist, form into a ball and, with a rolling pin dusted with flour, on a lightly floured surface roll out from center until it is ⅛ inch thick.

3. Press into pie plate; trim edges ½ inch beyond rim.

4. With your thumb and index fingers pinch edges around dish to make scallops. Set pie shell aside.

5. *TO PREPARE FILLING:* In a large bowl, combine vanilla, brown sugar, cornstarch, pumpkin pie spice, pumpkin, and condensed milk. With a wooden spoon, stir until completely mixed. Pour into unbaked pie shell.

6. Bake for 55 to 60 minutes until knife inserted in center comes out clean.

7. Cool on wire rack and refrigerate for 1 hour before serving.

Variation
For a very sweet pie, add ¼ cup brown sugar.

Peach-Blueberry Cobbler

4 cups peeled sliced peaches

1 pint fresh blueberries

¾ cup sugar

2 tablespoons cornstarch

2 tablespoons water

½ teaspoon grated lemon peel

1 tablespoon lemon juice

PASTRY

1 cup unbleached all-purpose
flour

2 tablespoons sugar

1½ teaspoons baking powder

⅛ teaspoon salt

¼ cup butter or margarine, room
temperature

½ cup heavy cream or whipping
cream

This cobbler is a dream come true—easy, great-tasting, and beautiful-looking.

1. In a medium saucepan, combine peaches, blueberries, sugar, cornstarch, and water and allow to come to a boil for 1 minute; remove from burner and stir in lemon peel and lemon juice.

2. Pour out into a 9-inch square pan. Preheat oven to 425°F.

3. *TO PREPARE PASTRY:* In a large bowl, mix flour, 1 tablespoon sugar, baking powder, and salt. With a pastry blender, cut in butter or margarine until mixture resembles course crumbs. Stir in cream. Knead in bowl a few times until smooth dough forms.

4. Turn out dough onto a lightly floured surface and with a floured rolling pin, roll into a 9-inch square and place over fruit in pan. Sprinkle with remaining sugar.

5. Place baking dish on cookie sheet and bake for 20 to 25 minutes.

Cinnamon Beignets

Vegetable oil for deep frying

1½ cups unbleached flour

⅓ cup sugar

3½ teaspoons baking powder

¼ teaspoon salt

1½ teaspoons vanilla extract

¼ teaspoon ground cinnamon

¼ teaspoon ground nutmeg

¾ cup milk

1½ tablespoons lemon juice

2 tablespoons vegetable oil

TOPPING

½ cup sugar

1 teaspoon ground cinnamon

These are an extra-special treat to serve at brunch or as a snack or at breakfast.

1. Into a medium saucepan, pour 3½ inches of oil and set aside.

2. In a large bowl, combine flour, sugar, baking powder, salt, vanilla, cinnamon, nutmeg, milk, lemon juice, and oil. Stir until dry ingredients are moistened. (If batter is too moist, add a little more flour.)

3. Heat oil in saucepan to 375°F. Drop a piece of cubed bread into hot oil; when bread browns in 50 seconds, oil is ready for frying. Take out bread.

4. Drop 1 teaspoonful batter at a time into oil; deep fry only three at a time. Keep checking thermometer. (If oil is hot enough, the doughnut will not absorb any oil; if oil is too hot, it will smoke and doughnuts will brown on outside and not cook on inside.)

5. Fry doughnut drops approximately 1 minute or until they rise to the top; then turn them over and fry other side until golden brown. Take out with a slotted spoon. Drain off excess oil on paper towels.

6. *TO PREPARE TOPPING:* In a flat platter, mix sugar and cinnamon together and roll each warm doughnut in mixture to coat.

Delicious Doughnuts

½ cup milk

½ cup granulated sugar

1 (¼-ounce) package active dry yeast

¾ stick unsalted butter, softened

½ teaspoon ground nutmeg

3¼ cups unbleached all-purpose flour

Vegetable oil for deep frying

SUGAR GLAZE

2 cups sifted confectioners' sugar

1½ teaspoons vanilla extract

⅓ cup water

COATING

1 cup sugar

2¼ teaspoons ground cinnamon

These doughnuts are light, tasty, and airy. They are a must-try.

1. In a medium saucepan, heat milk on medium setting to luke-warm.

2. Into a large bowl, pour milk. Add sugar and stir in yeast; let stand 5 minutes or until foamy. Add butter and nutmeg and whisk until combined (will have butter lumps). Add 2 cups of flour, beat with a handheld electric mixer set on medium speed, for 2 minutes or until batter is smooth. Slowly add remaining flour to form soft dough (if dough is too sticky add a little more flour).

3. Turn out dough onto a lightly floured surface and knead for 5 to 6 minutes until smooth.

4. Place dough into a medium bowl lightly coated with oil, then turn it so top is coated also; cover it with a cloth and let rise in a warm place for 1 to 1½ hours or until double in size.

5. Punch down dough and turn out onto a floured surface. With a rolling pin, roll dough out to one-half-inch thickness. Cut out doughnuts with a 2½-inch floured doughnut cutter or a floured round glass. Transfer them and their holes to a sheet of wax paper.

6. Knead remaining dough back into a ball and make more doughnuts by repeating step 5. Allow the doughnuts and their holes to rise, covered, in a warm place for 1 hour or until they double in size.

7. *TO PREPARE GLAZE:* Meanwhile, to a small bowl, add confectioners' sugar, vanilla, and water; whisk ingredients together until smooth, adding more water if necessary. Set aside.

8. *TO PREPARE CINNAMON SUGAR COATING:* Meanwhile, on a serving platter, mix sugar and cinnamon together. Set aside.

9. After doughnuts have risen; they are now ready for frying.

10. In a large saucepan, fill to 2 inches with oil. Heat oil to 375°F. Drop a piece of cubed bread into hot oil; when bread browns in 50 seconds, the oil is ready for frying. Take out bread.

11. Drop 4 to 5 doughnuts and holes in at a time, turning them as they rise to the surface; fry 2 to 3 minutes until both sides are golden brown. Keep checking thermometer.

12. With a spoon with holes in it, transfer doughnuts and holes to paper towels to drain.

13. While doughnuts are still warm, dip tops and holes in glaze or roll them in cinnamon-sugar mixture. Dry the glazed ones 5 minutes on wire racks.

Blueberry Apple Strudel

2 tablespoons unbleached all-
  purpose flour

1 teaspoon grated lemon rind

2 teaspoons lemon juice

2 tablespoons applesauce

1 teaspoon vanilla extract

1 teaspoon ground cinnamon

6 medium Cortland apples,
  peeled, cored, and thinly sliced

¼ cup firmly packed brown sugar

¼ cup granulated sugar

½ cup fresh blueberries

½ cup walnuts

8 sheets phyllo pastry dough

Approximately 2 tablespoons
  margarine or milk (to brush on
  top of phyllo)

Confectioners' sugar (to sprinkle
  on top)

This is crispy, and the combination of apple and blueberry is delicious.

1. In a large bowl, mix flour, lemon rind, lemon juice, apple-sauce, vanilla, cinnamon, sliced apples, and sugars. Fold in the blueberries and nuts.

2. Preheat oven to 350°F. Lightly butter a cookie sheet.

3. Place a sheet of phyllo dough on prepared cookie sheet. With a pastry brush, brush lightly with melted margarine, then place another sheet on top of that, coating each sheet in between with melted margarine until all 8 sheets are done. Then place apple mixture on top of pastry sheets evenly in center lengthwise leaving room on each side and ends to be able to seal. Fold side flaps over top and place seam on bottom (if it becomes too full, then just cut 2 more strips of phyllo and place them on top, brushing them with margarine and pressing with your fingers to seal). Seal ends by folding them under and turn to place seams on the bottom.

4. Brush top with a little melted margarine or milk for a golden shine.

5. Bake for approximately 30 minutes, or until golden brown. Let cool completely on wire rack.

Miscellaneous and Special Recipes

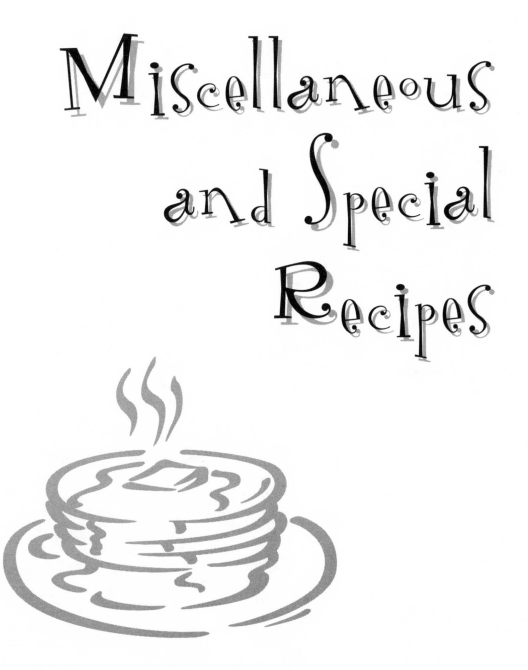

Pancakes or Waffles That Taste Great

makes approximately
8 medium pancakes or
4 large waffles

2 cups unbleached all-purpose
   flour

4 teaspoons baking powder

¼ teaspoon salt (optional)

3 tablespoons sugar

2 cups buttermilk

4 tablespoons oil or applesauce

½ teaspoon vanilla extract
   (optional)

Butter to cook (just enough to
   coat pan to fry pancakes)

These pancakes or waffles can be frozen, and they are especially great with a little of your favorite fruit in them.

1. In a small bowl, combine flour, baking powder, salt (if used), sugar, milk, oil or applesauce, and vanilla (if used). Whisk together until smooth.

2. *PANCAKE COOKING DIRECTIONS:* In a large skillet on medium heat, melt butter and brown pancakes on both sides just as you would any other pancakes.

3. *WAFFLE COOKING DIRECTIONS:* Heat a non-stick–coated waffle iron and follow griddle directions as you would for any other waffle.

Variations

Substitute soy milk for the buttermilk if you cannot have milk. Add ½ cup of either blueberries, strawberries, peaches, or apples.

Caroline's Chocolate Glass-Bowl Dessert

1 (8-ounce) package light cream
cheese, room temperature

1 cup sifted confectioners' sugar

2 (3.5-ounce) packages vanilla
instant pudding mix

2 teaspoons coffee liqueur

3½ cups milk

12 ounces whipped cream

2½ cup crushed chocolate cookie
crumbs

1 teaspoon instant coffee
granules

1 teaspoon vanilla extract

This is a really fun little dessert for children to make and eat. It is off the chart on the sweet meter.

1. In a large bowl, combine light cream cheese and confectioners' sugar. With a handheld electric mixer set on medium speed, beat for 3 minutes until fluffy. Add pudding, coffee liqueur, and milk and beat for another 3 minutes until thick; gently fold in previously whipped cream just until combined. Set aside.

2. In a small bowl, combine pre-crushed chocolate crumbs, coffee granules, and vanilla. Set aside.

3. *TO ASSEMBLE DESSERT:* Evenly line bottom of a medium glass bowl with a third of chocolate crumb mixture. Spoon out half of cream cheese mixture evenly over crumb mixture. Sprinkle on another third of cookie crumb mixture, and spoon out remaining cream cheese mixture evenly over that. Then finally sprinkle remaining cookie crumb mixture on top.

4. Refrigerate overnight. Serve cold.

Cream Cheese, White Chocolate, Glass-Bowl Dessert

serves 12 to 16

This is one of my brother's favorite desserts. You'll see why.

CRUST

2 cups graham cracker crumbs

½ cup margarine, melted

2 tablespoons sugar

FILLING

1 (10-ounce) package white chocolate chips

⅓ cup whipping cream

1 (8-ounce) package cream cheese, room temperature

2 bananas sliced

TOPPING

1 (3.4-ounce) package vanilla or chocolate instant pudding and pie filling

2 cups assorted sliced fresh or canned fruit of your choice

Whipped cream (optional)

1. *TO PREPARE CRUST:* In a medium bowl, combine cracker crumbs, melted margarine, and sugar; mix well.

2. *TO PREPARE FILLING:* In microwave-safe bowl, combine white chocolate and whipping cream. Cover with plastic wrap with a couple of holes punched in it. Place in microwave on high setting for 1 to 1½ minutes or until chips melt and mixture is smooth when stirred. With a handheld electric mixer set on medium speed, beat in cream cheese for 3 minutes until smooth.

3. *TO ASSEMBLE DESSERT:* Press 1 cup of graham cracker crumb mixture into bottom of a 9-inch-tall or trifle glass bowl (reserve 1 cup).

4. Layer half of white chocolate–cream cheese mixture over graham cracker crumbs, spreading evenly with a spatula. Layer evenly with sliced bananas.

5. Sprinkle evenly half of remaining reserved graham cracker mixture over bananas.

6. Layer remaining half of white chocolate–cream cheese mixture over that, spreading evenly with a spatula.

7. *TO PREPARE TOPPING:* Prepare vanilla or chocolate pudding, according to package directions. Spoon out vanilla or chocolate pudding evenly over white chocolate–cream cheese mixture.

8. Layer sliced fruit evenly over top and cover with dollops of whipped cream.

Beer Batter

2 cups unbleached all-purpose
  flour

1½ cups flat beer

1 teaspoon baking powder

Oil for frying

This recipe is good for fruit or vegetables. It is very delicious for those of you who want something you thought you could make only with eggs.

1. In a large bowl, combine flour, beer, and baking powder until mixture forms a batter.

2. Then you can slice up your favorite fruit or veggies and coat with batter.

3. Fill a large saucepan with 1 inch of oil and heat on high to 375°F.

4. Then, deep fry veggies or fruit until golden brown.

5. Remove with a slotted spoon onto paper towels to drain oil.

Index